Anna G. Shillabeer

The Health of Vietnam

Springer

Anna G. Shillabeer
CSEM, Flinders University
Adelaide, SA, Australia

ISBN 978-981-10-1274-7 ISBN 978-981-287-709-3 (eBook)
DOI 10.1007/978-981-287-709-3

Springer Singapore Heidelberg New York Dordrecht London

Softcover re-print of the Hardcover 1st edition 2016

Printed on acid-free paper

Springer Science+Business Media Singapore Pte Ltd. is part of Springer Science+Business Media (www.springer.com)

This book is dedicated to Callan, Declan,
Aydan, Zoe and the health of all Vietnamese.

Contents

List of Figures

List of Tables

Chapter 1
Introduction

Welcome to Viet Nam, a country whose people are resilient, resourceful, culturally diverse, innovative, entrepreneurial and very proud. It is a country whose population recently hit 90 million but where over 25,000 children die from cancer each year that would not die in Canada, Australia, Germany or other developed countries, where countless more children die in utero or soon after birth because mothers are not empowered with basic health knowledge or support to provide the best possible care for their pregnancy or baby, and where two or three patients sharing a hospital bed including in chronic care and intensive treatment environments is not uncommon. It is also a country with very little health data capacity and where almost no information systems are implemented effectively or provide any capacity to facilitate whole of patient care enablement or evidence-based decision-making in clinical management.

The Vietnamese public health environment is undergoing significant policy and clinical change. Viet Nam has been at war for most of the past 150 years either internally or externally with the most recent war ending in the mid-1970s. Health policy and spending were almost zero until the 1980s. This history has presented a complex scenario in which to develop structures and deliver healthcare services to the population. The healthcare environment has progressed little beyond the greenfield stage in terms of innovation, evidence-based practice and service delivery. There are many endemic issues not seen in other geographies and few solutions have been implemented. One major barrier to the application of any form of evidence-driven healthcare is the lack of consistent, clean and structured data. Systems are too often little more than data collection points that are used to input incomplete data, frustrate medical professionals and negatively impact upon the potential for health analysts and policymakers to provide value where it is critically needed. Changes to healthcare policy and structure are guided by a 5-year plan which is an independently analysed ministerial document. The plan documents progress realised from the previous iteration, the current state of healthcare categorised by WHO metrics, and outlines the activities and investment to address the areas of greatest need for the future (Fig. 1.1).

A.G. Shillabeer, *The Health of Vietnam*, DOI 10.1007/978-981-287-709-3_1

Fig. 1.1 Map of Viet Nam showing provinces and cities [2]

There is a multifaceted migration factor complicating the environment and exacerbating the landscape. Many doctors seek higher wages and better conditions by working in city hospitals and clinics. As a result of the lack of specialists in rural areas in particular, many patients are required to move (often against their family's wishes) into a city for treatment. In patient terms this relocation increases trauma and anxiety as individuals are out of their hometown and away from families who are their usual avenue of support. This professional and patient migration also exacerbates the problem of overcrowding in city hospitals and reduces investment and service provision in rural health thus creating a vicious circle.

Whilst there are clear areas for improvement, Viet Nam is also a country plagued and somewhat limited by misconceptions and innuendo. There are many that immediately conjure up images of a war-torn country with little or no facilities; however, this is very much an identity of the past and although many local Vietnamese are troubled by their memories, it is their knowledge that this is how Viet Nam is perceived that troubles them more. Several international websites, especially linked to tourism information, are still propagating this perception, for example, the following exert from an American tourism website:

> The following may be issues relevant to travel to Viet Nam:
>
> Adequate medical care is available in Hanoi, Ho Chi Minh City, and Vung Tau, but is substandard throughout the rest of the country, hospital beds are limited and modern technology is lacking. [1]

Whilst there is a disclaimer on this information that it 'may be out of date', it was certainly already well out of date by June 2014. It is possible to get very high-quality healthcare services and treatments in Viet Nam and medical training programmes are well structured and comparable with those in the west.

Viet Nam is a relatively poor country. It has recently been promoted out of Third World status; however, the average per capita income is still less than $2000 a year. This has myriad of impacts on healthcare not the least of which is affordability. There are significant financial constraints both in terms of access to world-class treatments and services for the average Vietnamese and in terms of compliance to long-term treatment protocols. One lost wage to a family can be critical to their well-being and survival and hence the primary aim of a Vietnamese patient is to return to work as soon as possible, even if not fully recovered. This presents barriers to realising good outcomes and places a significant burden on doctors, healthcare providers and policymakers to ensure that healthcare is affordable and accessible to all and that patients understand that full recovery is the most beneficial for them in the long run. There is a culturally diverse and complex environment in Viet Nam with both social and religious factors to consider in understanding why the healthcare systems and outcomes in Viet Nam are as they are. The origins of modern Viet Nam can be traced back 5000 years and there is a lot of history and embedded belief to overcome before major change can be realised.

This book aims to provide a broad overview of the Vietnamese healthcare environment. There has been little written on this topic but many are endeavouring to work in the country to develop or support health-focused initiatives. This book will inform, guide and objectively draw a detailed picture of the healthcare sector including history, policy, reforms, technology, treatments, stakeholders and areas for future focus. There are millions of well-intentioned dollars spent by international researchers and health groups, and whilst many demonstrate that improvements can be realised and measured, little local empowerment and therefore sustainability have been realised. This is partly due to the current fragmented approach, partly because of a lack of full understanding about where to best target the resources and partly due to political or cultural barriers.

The key foci for future healthcare capacity improvement are greater investment in technology and training for key areas of future need, a whole of country strategic approach to encouraging overseas investment with a requirement for capacity building at the local level, educating the general population of Viet Nam about their general health and implementing a programme to inform all patients about their diagnosis and treatment options during a consultation. This would enable earlier diagnoses, higher compliance, better prognoses and often shorter treatments which will ease the burden on hospital beds and reduce the long-term costs.

This book will be a unique presentation that provides a valuable insight into a largely hidden public health context.

References

1. www.rightdiagnosis.com/travel-health/Vietnam.htm posted 17th June 2014. Accessed 5 Oct 2014
2. Viet Nam Institute of Architecture, Urban and Rural Planning (VIAP) website. www.mlit.go.jp/kokudokeikaku/international/spw/general/vietnam/index_e.html. Accessed 12 Dec 2014

Chapter 2
The Vietnamese Healthcare Landscape

2.1 Brief History of Healthcare in Viet Nam

The history of Viet Nam has been bloody for many generations resulting in a consistently young population. Close to two thirds of the country's 90 million people are under the age of 35 years but, given that peace has come to Viet Nam, it is now naturally aging. This has meant that a very skewed healthcare environment has developed. There has been an emphasis on managing illness of the young or early onset conditions, accidents, combat-related injury, communicable disease, asthma, sexually transmitted diseases, etc. There has been little need to focus on disease of the aging or elderly, dementia, arthritis, degenerative disease, frailty, etc. There is limited experience in treating an aging population, and this significantly impacts on the provision of quality healthcare service for the population. It also means that elders have not been available to inform, educate and share health knowledge in areas such as pregnancy, child care, nutrition and general personal health management as occurs in the west.

The annual GDP has been growing at 6–8 % annually since 2000 leading to Viet Nam being recently promoted to lower-middle-income status. Whilst this would generally be considered a positive and beneficial transition, it is reportedly triggering the withdrawal of foreign aid, most notably in the health sector [1]. For the first time, the Vietnamese are developing a disposable income and the use of this is heavily influenced by their exposure to the western media and products. Their growing attraction to, and emulation of, the western lifestyle has led to the development of bad habits which further stress the inexperienced health system. Viet Nam is now experiencing a growing incidence of lung disease, cardiovascular disease, stress, diabetes, obesity, cancer and other diseases of the west that are driven by a consumer lifestyle. These are not conditions that have a treatment history or which have a population of experienced clinicians waiting to treat new cases. The history of healthcare drivers in Viet Nam has been relatively static over recent centuries, and treatments have been similarly consistent. This is now changing, and it is with some trepidation that Vietnamese healthcare providers and policymakers look to the new

A.G. Shillabeer, *The Health of Vietnam*, DOI 10.1007/978-981-287-709-3_2

landscape and try to provide the best possible service for a rapidly changing set of needs and drivers. This change has been realised in a single generation and Viet Nam has yet to demonstrate that it can manage and address this huge shift in priorities.

According to 2009 statistics, Viet Nam has 63 provinces, 687 cities and districts and 11,035 communes [1]. Seventy percent of the population live in rural areas and represent a number of separate cultures each with their own beliefs, some of which are very isolated such as the Hmong people in the northern hills area. The lifestyle, beliefs and healthcare drivers have remained relatively unchanged for many generations. Many have little or no access to modern healthcare facilities or clinicians, so the traditional ways are retained as a primary resource for those people. Healthcare provision and knowledge across rural Viet Nam are frequently received through community elders, where they exist, and family. This results in fragmented populations and practices. A significant proportion of rural people are also very poor (Viet Nam's per capita income was $1730 in 2012 [2]), and they cannot afford high-quality treatments or insurance policies even where they are available. There are less choices in healthcare providers and fewer specialised healthcare services and practitioners available in rural areas thus impacting upon the effectiveness of treatments which leads to a lack of trust in modern medicine, further driving the population away from clinics and reducing the demand and hence the funding to support such institutions in general. 2012 statistics from the Viet Nam Association of Paediatrics showed that 50 % of hospitalised newborns died within 1 day of being admitted for emergency treatment because they did not receive proper emergency aid at lower-level hospitals [3]. This creates a vicious circle from which it is near impossible to break free and which ensures a general lack of progress in healthcare over time.

The story is, of course, very different in urban areas where the demand for service, both in terms of quality and range, is growing and where salaries and availability of technical infrastructure for specialised practitioners are increasing. This practice environment makes urban practice much more attractive than rural, which in turn further exacerbates the rural healthcare crisis [4].

The growing demand for service in urban areas is however outstripping the ability to grow the sector and leads to its own endemic problems. Even when a patient is diagnosed and admitted for treatment after days of waiting for tests and results, too often their situation does not improve. As a direct result of the misalignment between growth in demand and ability of the system to evolve, hospitals are very overcrowded and understaffed across the country. Many patients reportedly cannot even assume basic rights as there are not enough beds to allow for one for each patient and doctors see on average 100 patients every day and hence often do not have time to even inform patients of their diagnosis or treatment options [5]. Recent work with the Ho Chi Minh Cancer Hospital revealed that there were up to 300 new diagnoses per day, an average of greater than 2 patients per bed, 10,000 outpatients to be managed and long queues waiting in hot buildings or sitting on floors outside or in stairwells and, most alarmingly, less than 60 % of patients are told their diagnosis. These observations are unfortunately not isolated to one city or hospital [5] (Figs. 2.1 and 2.2).

Fig. 2.1 A patient undergoing chemotherapy sits outside their overcrowded ward

Human resources for health (HRH) are limited and imbalanced [6]; there are 34.7 health workers per 10,000 people, among whom 6.5 are medical doctors, 1.2 are pharmacists and 8 are nurses [7]. According to a 2006 WHO report, HRH in Viet Nam is about half the number in other countries in the region [7]. The attraction of a medical degree is far lower than in most western countries where for most it would be the degree of choice given the potential career and income benefits over the term of the life. In Viet Nam even specialists often earn little more than $400 per month in the public sector (required placement for the first 5 years of practice) and hence are forced to work privately out of hours to support their extended family [8, 9]. The degree is longer than for other fields and the potential for a return on that investment is low. In contrast a student can complete an IT diploma or degree in 2–3 years and be earning up to $600 a month on graduation. Whilst culturally respected, medicine is not a profession for those that do not have a calling and who are not willing to work long hours for little recompense.

Fig. 2.2 A cancer patient is assisted to walk across a bridge to receive radiology services

The healthcare system has at best a tenuous ability to adequately meet the needs of the people it is designed to serve. This presents a very complex and unconstrained environment in which to introduce any new population health initiative.

2.2 The Vietnamese Healthcare Delivery Platform

The formal healthcare system in Viet Nam has a four-tiered healthcare model as shown in Fig. 2.3. The country has 1030 public hospitals, with more than 128,000 beds, and 62 private hospitals [5].

Patients usually seek a primary assessment within a commune-level healthcare institution and are then referred up through the tiers until they reach a national hospital which specialises in the treatment of a particular serious or chronic illness such as late-stage renal failure, AIDS or cancer if relevant. Some patients may move several times from their rural homeland until they are admitted for treatment. This can take months and cover great distances resulting in dislocation and isolation. Vietnamese culture is very strongly family oriented, and hence the potential for dislocation in particular is a significant deterrent to accessing modern healthcare services even if available.

Limited palliative care support services are available in the national hospitals but this is not a common practice and demand for such services is not part of the health landscape for most. Those with a terminal diagnosis will generally return home to spend their remaining time being cared for by family. The Ho Chi Minh Cancer Hospital, for example, has 8 palliative beds available as of 2014 for over 10,000 patients and is the only hospital with specialised palliative care provision. To put this into perspective, we should consider that of the approximate 125,000 diagnoses of cancer per year, almost 95,000 will die [10]. Therefore, the real coverage is 8 beds per 95,000 terminal cancer patients or <1 per 10,000. To equate with the

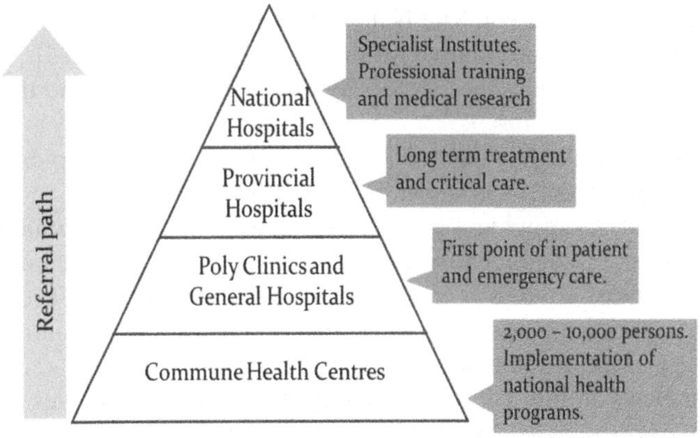

Fig. 2.3 The four-tiered Vietnamese healthcare structure [5]

Table 2.1 Healthcare governance and management structure [16]

Stakeholders	Governance	Authority
System level: Ministry of Health (MOH)		
16 departments, administrations, cabinet	Self	Development of national directives, strategic plans and policy. National budget disbursement to priority areas, healthcare training and research and specialised public services
36 central hospitals		
17 institutes or centres		
14 schools or colleges		
System level: provincial health services		
230 provincial hospitals	Technical guidance from MOH	Disbursement of budget to local priority areas and organisations. Development of local targets and priorities
63 preventive health centres		
Local medical schools or colleges if applicable		
System level: district health office		
690 district preventive health centres	Direct management from provincial health services and technical guidance from provincial stakeholders	None
734 district hospitals and polyclinics		
System level: communal health stations		
Small clinics and community health outposts	Direct management from district health services and technical guidance from district stakeholders	None

Vietnamese context, there is also <1 bed per 10,000 terminal cancer patients in Ireland, Australia, Denmark and a number of other western countries [11–13].

This suggests that Viet Nam is keeping pace with the world; however, almost every other developed country has a home care or hospice service that caters for an average of 45 % of dying cancer patients [14]. This level of service is only known to exist through one facility in Viet Nam run by an international doctor who saw a huge gap, but the cost is prohibitive for the average Vietnamese [15]. Tens of thousands do not receive, or have access to, any end-of-life care beyond their untrained family.

Governance over the Vietnamese healthcare system has a top-down structure with delegated management as shown in Table 2.1 [16].

Tables 2.2 and 2.3 provide a comparative overview of the Vietnamese context against other locations and identify a number of foci for healthcare improvement in Viet Nam. The most obvious is maternal and child health where according to the CIA, Viet Nam is doing better than many other Southeast Asian countries but is well behind the rest of the developed world [18].

Viet Nam News on July 11, 2012, reported that whilst the statistics had improved dramatically over the past 12 years, there was still a significant difference between

Table 2.2 Comparison of healthcare environments (Southeast Asia) [17, 18]

Context	Viet Nam	Thailand	Laos	Indonesia	Philippines
Urbanisation %	30	34	33	44	49
Health workers per 1000	1.22	0.3	0.27	0.29	1.15
Maternal deaths per 100 k	59	48	470	220	99
Child mortality per 1000	19.61	15.41	56.13	20.06	18.19
Health spend as % of GDP	7.2	3.9	4.5	2.6	3.6
Hospital beds per 1000	3.1	2.1	0.7	0.6	0.5
Years of education/literacy	10/94	12/92.6	9/73	13	12/92.6
Life expectancy	75.2	74	67.9	69.5	69.4
Heart disease	78,352	53,328	6679	243,048	57,864
HIV/AIDS	13,655	29,255	93	6418	172
Diabetes mellitus	16,456	35,787	636	48,294	18,512
Asthma	8084	1519	223	14,624	10,471
Cancer	74,457	66,098	3520	171,879	39,952
Diarrhoea	3013	7987	1281	30,328	6828
Road trauma	21,087	28,778	1059	48,074	8175

Table 2.3 Comparison of healthcare environment (world) statistics [17–21]

Context	Viet Nam	Australia	Norway	America	World
Urbanisation %	30	89	79	82	52.1
Health workers per 1000	1.22	3	4.1	2.7	1.39
Maternal deaths per 100 k	59	8	7	24	210
Child mortality per 1000	19.61	4.55	3.5	5.98	36.58
Health spend as % of GDP	7.2	8.5	9.7	16.2	10.1
Hospital beds per 1000	3.1	3.82	3.52	3.1	2.9
Years of education/literacy	10/94	21/99	17/100	16/99	12/84.1
Life expectancy	75.2	82.2	81.4	78.6	68.9
Heart disease	78,352	24,905	6008	445,864	7,253,824
HIV/AIDS	13,655	107	14	11,630	1,776,270
Diabetes	16,456	3871	742	75,280	1,255,477
Asthma	8084	438	117	3653	284,046
Cancer	74,457	35,635	10,094	538,471	6,699,490
Diarrhoea	3013	84	235	7298	2,464,425
Road trauma	21,087	1456	257	45,154	1,208,629

urban and rural rates of maternal and newborn deaths. This is believed to be due to limited access to healthcare and far lower rates of trained obstetricians in rural areas compared to cities [5]. This is identified as an area for greater investment by the government and presents a viable area of focus for research in this country.

2.3 Traditional Healthcare

The history of healthcare in Viet Nam is long, and many date it from around 1780 with Le Huu Trac (also known as Hai Thuong Lan Ong) [22]. He is considered to be the grandfather of medicine in Viet Nam and was the first to document traditional medicine. Previously there were only texts on Chinese medicine, but Viet Nam has its own legacy of plants and animals used for medicinal purposes, many of which are still applied as a first-line medical intervention or for those otherwise incurable with modern medicine.

Hai Thuong Lan Ong was a physician and an academic and spent the last 10 years of his life writing books on therapies and treatments both medicinal and physical in nature. He died at age 51 [22, 23]. Ong's texts were written in an old script that is no longer used and unfortunately many of his works were not translated and have been lost. Thankfully and surprisingly, most of those that were not lost survived the tumultuous history of events and have been translated into modern Vietnamese and digitised in many cases. Those original texts that do still exist reside in medical libraries in Viet Nam's top universities and remain on the list of core texts in universities offering traditional medicine teaching [23].

The dichotomy between traditional and modern medicine is no better demonstrated than on the streets where a very modern-style pharmacy, filled with packets and formulated commercial products, sits alongside very traditional pharmaceutical providers with rows of jars filled with unrecognisable substances each individually selected and combined to meet the needs of an individual customer. Ingredients such as fungi, roots, stems, leaves and flowers are dried in open baskets and then processed and combined on the footpath by white-coated 'alchemists' sitting on commonly seen small plastic stools (Fig. 2.4).

Traditional treatment structures and practices are so strongly embedded in the cultural psyche that even when Vietnamese migrate to other countries, they will often shun the practices of their new home in favour of traditional therapies until it is absolutely necessary to seek help [24]. Interestingly, several of these traditional practices are experiencing popularity in western countries, especially with celebrities in Hollywood looking for something new [25].

Some of the more common healing techniques include [24]:

- Coining – a coin dipped in mentholated oil is vigorously rubbed across the skin in a specifically taught manner. The location for this is often the neck, shoulders or arms and it causes a mild surface abrasion and/or bruise. This practice is believed to restore balance and allow bad forces to be released.
- Cupping – heated glasses similar to small bowls are placed on the skin, forming a suction effect that leaves a visible red circular mark, sometimes lasting days. This process is believed to draw out the bad forces or pollutants from within the body that are causing illness or discomfort.
- Pinching – the skin is pinched repeatedly which results in a bruise or surface abrasion. This is believed to provide a mechanism by which the causative agent can exit the body.

Fig. 2.4 A Hanoi traditional medicine street pharmacy with pharmacists in the background

- Steaming – a specifically selected combination of medicinal herbs is boiled in water, and then the steam is inhaled. Often full body immersion is prescribed also.
- Balm – various medicated oils or balms are made from flora- and fauna-based products and used externally either on specific areas or for broad dermatological conditions rubbed over the whole skin.
- Acupuncture – specialised natural practitioners insert very fine steel needles into specific locations on the skin known as vital-energy points. Each of these points is believed to have specific therapeutic effects and each is connected through energy lines to internal organs or muscular structures. These energy lines are documented and are still studied as part of some university courses. See Fig. 2.5 showing the many points on the ear and their corresponding organ relationship. This demonstrates the complexity and length of study required for some traditional practitioners.
- Acupressure or massage – very precise digital pressure is applied at defined acupuncture points rather than inserting needles. This may be combined with massage to further stimulate these points and maximise their therapeutic effects.
- Herbs – natural plant-based remedies are very commonly provided by pharmacists practising according to traditional formulae. Medicinal herbs are selected and often boiled in water or mixed with a carrier such as 'wine' and consumed.
- Patent medicines – commercial powdered medicines are mixed or boiled with water and taken to dilute them and reduce the negative effects that are believed to be associated. This is especially true of medicines that may cause side effects such as nausea.

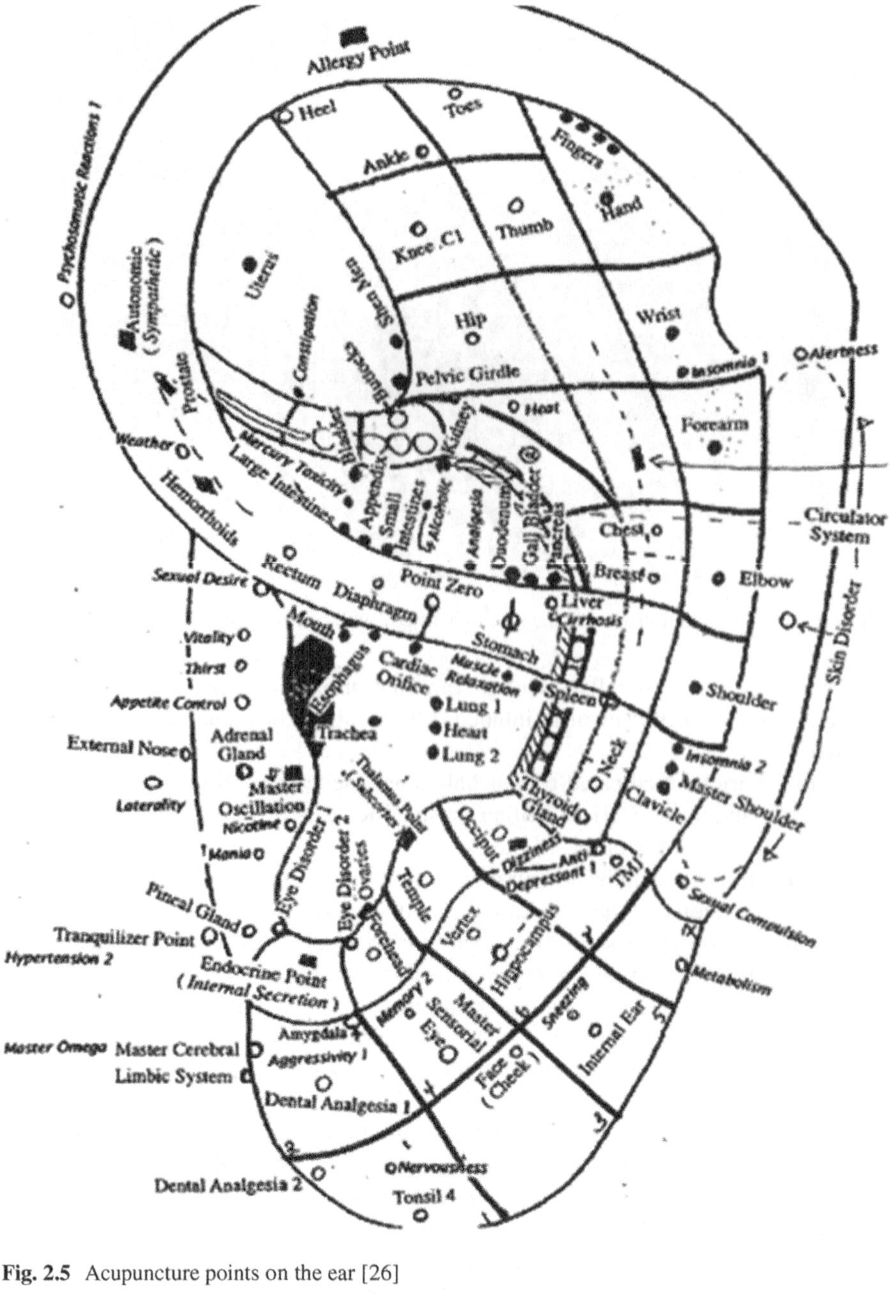

Fig. 2.5 Acupuncture points on the ear [26]

2.4 Auxiliary and Community Healthcare Services

In Viet Nam the concept of social care is unknown, at least within local jurisdictions. Any visible social care initiatives are implemented by international organisations. This is primarily due to the very different family structures that exist in the cultural context. In Viet Nam the family is at the centre of any health and welfare need of family members. If someone needs support then it is provided by the family, no matter what the burden or cost. There is therefore little or no demand for social welfare services as seen in western countries. This does not however mean that there is no need, far from it. Key areas for potential support services include child and maternal health, disability assistance, mental health, health literacy improvement, chronic health condition management and aged care.

Child and maternal health is an area of focus for the Vietnamese Government. The number of pregnancies is growing as the population grows, and hence there are more and more women looking for medical services especially in the growing urban areas such as Ho Chi Minh City, Hanoi and Da Nang. This presents issues in terms of quality and quantity of care provided. The number of pregnancies is growing faster than the graduation of required numbers of doctors to care for them. As with many chronic diseases, this means that each patient gets to spend less and less time with their doctor and receives less and less information. There are anecdotal stories of the impact of this lack of information and support. One such story was from a father who was extremely worried that his 5-week-old baby was going to die as for a number of nights it had not woken up for its usual feed. It had slept between 10 pm and 5 am, but the parents had not! When asked if the baby woke up by itself and was hungry in the morning, the father replied ‘yes, the baby is very hungry and drinks a lot’. It had to be explained that this was perfectly normal and he and his wife should enjoy having a good baby and above all else get some sleep whilst the opportunity presented. There are also many stories about women not knowing what the tests they had to have were for and again worrying that something may be wrong. Women also revealed that they were taking unknown supplements that they had been told were good but they had no knowledge regarding the content or supposed effects. The need for better ante- and postnatal support and education and health literacy programmes is self-evident in this domain.

Aged care is singled out as anecdotal evidence which again suggests that foreign researchers often assume that there would be aged-care institutions in Viet Nam as in other countries around the world. This again shows that research and health project foundations must be based on an understanding of the cultural and religious underpinnings of the societal structures. In particular developing an understanding of the Confucian philosophy and beliefs that are held by most Vietnamese is critical to being able to facilitate project management structures and deliver outcomes. In the context of aged care, the elder members of the family are deeply respected and are cared for in the family home for the term of their life, not in an institution regardless of their health or other issues as seen in western countries. The oldest son usually resides with his parents and brings his wife to live in that home. It is her that will usually care for the parents, whilst he works. Often the wife will work also but maintains significant responsibilities in the house. This is another story entirely. The concept of aged homes is simply not evident in Viet Nam. Families would simply not consider such an option. It would be seen as losing face which is to be avoided at all costs. There is little specialist medical care or training in aged care, and this presents an obvious issue for Viet Nam which is gradually regaining an older generation but with little experience in treating or supporting conditions such as failing sensory awareness, Alzheimer's and arthritis that are more commonly found in older generations. Those with greatest need are therefore being cared for by those with least capability or capacity.

In all of this we must of course be cognisant of the flow on problems that would be caused by enforcing or providing a westernised opinion or healthcare structure as this will not be well accepted. We cannot simply open an aged-care facility, no matter what the benefits may be, and expect that this will be accepted. It could instead be seen as deeply insulting to suggest that families are not properly caring for their elders. It must be a process of identifying where the greatest good can be achieved and then determining a culturally sensitive way to effect and sustain change. If the solution is not seen as acceptable, then locals will not be open to engaging and any benefits will not be sustained.

Mental health support is an area where there is a critical need as it does not follow the same pattern as other conditions that affect a family [27]. Having a mental health issue is seen as bringing shame on the family and often the whole community in which the person lives. It is believed that if a person has such an illness, then the family must be cursed or has some terrible inherent weakness at best. The whole family would commonly be cut off by the community to prevent others from becoming tainted by association. The result of this is either that a family will live in total isolation and need to become self-sufficient or they rid themselves of the 'cursed one' and send them to an institution. This would seem to have some similarities with western practices where those with serious mental health issues are often shunned, institutionalised and forgotten. The main difference however is that mental health facilities in Viet Nam are not pristine hospitals with 24/7/365 specialised professional care and attendance; these are the very worst kind of institutions imaginable. They are crowded 'cells' with bars, often with no beds, effective medications or light where 'patients' may be chained up or left to writhe in their misery or be subject to violence by others in various psychotic states who are all pushed together. This is the stuff of horror movies, and those that have witnessed it said that the screams, distressed faces and anguished thrashing witnessed will haunt them forever. Institutions for the seriously ill are too often not places of treatment but the worst kind of incarceration.

The role of neighbouring countries is seen as having a huge potential to assist in developing care frameworks for Viet Nam. Korea in particular has a good relationship with Viet Nam but is seen as being a generation ahead in healthcare reform and Thailand is also showing positive gains in some areas such as maternal health that Viet Nam is still lagging behind in. There are also several areas where Viet Nam has management systems that Thailand and others can learn from. It would seem a waste of resources, time and money to continually reinvent the wheel every time a health scenario is identified as a focus in a country. There are research groups in Korea ready and willing to assist and share their experience. This highlights the need for a broader, regional approach to provide potential evidence-based solutions that can be trailed in Viet Nam and we should only move to develop something unique if this is not shown to be appropriate. Most importantly, Viet Nam's neighbours all have sufficiently similar beliefs and cultural philosophies, and as discussed here, there are some areas of immediate concern that could benefit from a regional, collaborative approach.

The concept of community care is therefore a gap in the healthcare continuum. Where it does exist it is minimal and restricted to the provision of community health services in commune clinics. Commune-level capacity and service provision is however at a critical low, and the personal and infrastructure ramifications are significant as discussed throughout this book. Commune-level health capacity improvement has been predominantly driven through collaborative initiatives by local universities as in the following two examples.

2.4.1 University Community Healthcare Initiatives

The military hospital and medical university stand alone in continuing to work on residual issues from the generations of war in Viet Nam. They engage in and have a number of collaborative projects which assist victims of Agent Orange/dioxin exposure [28]. They have been providing free advice and pharmaceutical treatment to sufferers in Ninh Binh Province and Da Nang. There have been broad detox programmes run through hospitals but these have not been specific for dioxin. One pilot programme run by the military hospital with 40 patients in the Da Nang Hospital evidenced that it is possible to reduce the levels of dioxin in blood by 30–60 % whilst also removing residuals of a number of other contaminants. The hospital Director, Major General Hoang Manh, declared that this trial evidenced the 'possibility to improve the quality of life for the victims' [28].

As an addition to this philanthropic effort, the hospital also has a foundation which provides financial support for those most affected by the chronic effects of chemical warfare exposure. The foundation has awarded interest-free 'gifts' to the value of $500,000 and has collaborated with a number of other philanthropic organisations to provide a further $65 million which is disbursed through the fund of the Association for Victims of Agent Orange/Dioxin in Ninh Binh [28].

Whilst the military hospital and university have provided community-level service delivery projects, Thai Nguyen University has focused on capacity-building projects [29]. In 5 years the university has graduated 100 masters students and over 350 undergraduate medical students and placed them into remote mountainous which have the lowest doctor/patient ratios and consequently the lowest levels of healthcare services. They have also opened up a large number of supported places for students from these remote and disadvantaged communities. Graduates from these low socio-economic areas are more likely to provide a sustained medical presence in their villages than those from more affluent or distant origins. Each year the school reserves close to 100 places for students who are children of ethnic minorities living in the mountainous areas of Ha Tinh [29].

2.4.2 *Auxiliary Health Services*

Auxiliary health services are also uncommon in Viet Nam and those that are offered are generally either by general practitioners through outpatient clinics in hospitals or too often by poorly trained and resourced private providers. Three cases are provided for demonstration: dental care, psychology and physiotherapy.

2.4.2.1 Dental Care

Dental care in Viet Nam is lacking and training and capacity development has been primarily driven by international organisations.

In 1997 a team from University of Maryland School of Dentistry began a programme of voluntary dental visits to Hanoi to provide dental care and treatment for up to 500 Vietnamese on each visit. They also imported supplies and expertise to assist in setting up a western-style dental school at the University of Hanoi. This became the first specialised dental school in Viet Nam [30].

Seven faculties of dentistry are now open in Viet Nam and are located in the following universities:

- Hanoi Medical University
- HCMC University of Medicine and Pharmacy
- Haiphong University
- Hue University
- Can Tho University
- Thai Nguyen University
- Tay Nguyen University (Central Highlands) [31].

The undergraduate dental degree takes 6 years to complete and is a specialisation in the standard medical degree. The dentistry programme offered by these universities was restructured in 2003 to provide more intensive training in dentistry for the students. Prior to the changes, the programme was composed of 4 years of standard medical sciences and 2 years of dental sciences. After 2003 the programme changed the balance between general and specialised content and is now structured with 3 years of medical sciences and 3 years of dental science [31].

A number of international research centres or projects have been implemented in Viet Nam including an oral health research centre opened in 2012 at the National Hospital of Odonto-Stomatology in Ho Chi Minh City. This is a collaborative initiative between the hospital and the Faculty of Dentistry at the University of British

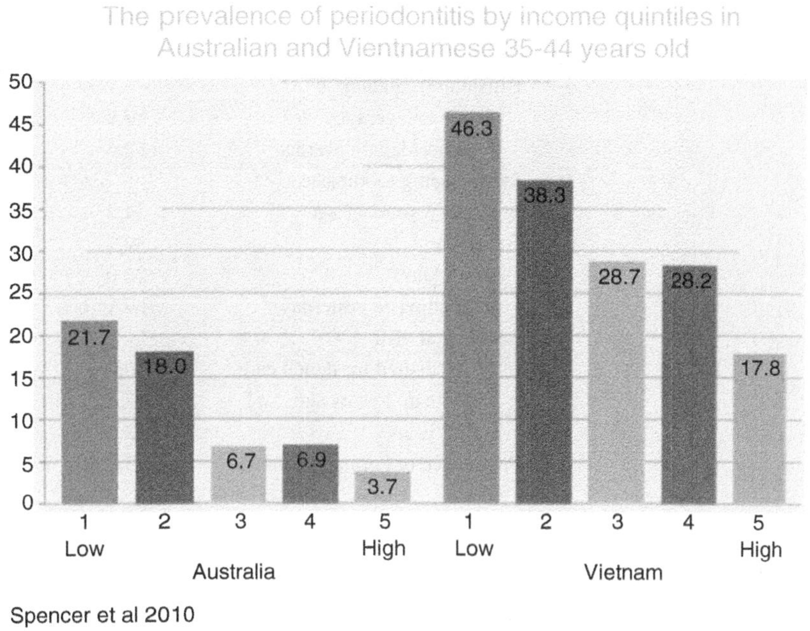

Fig. 2.6 Comparative periodontitis prevalence between Australia and Viet Nam [31]

Columbia, in Vancouver, Canada. This initiative was triggered by Operation Smile which is active across the developing world and engages volunteers to provide much needed dental services to many thousands of disadvantaged people. The aims of this group are to increase capacity in dental professionals and provide continuing education opportunities for dentists in Viet Nam [32].

More recently a joint project between Australian Research Centre for Population Oral Health and the University of Adelaide reported on the results of the second national survey of oral health of Viet Nam 1999–2000. The survey results showed that there was significant room for improvement in dental care in Viet Nam compared to other countries in the region. There were key differences in number of caries in both children and adults, in access to dental services and in periodontitis prevalence as shown in Fig. 2.6 [31]. A clear determinant in dental health issues is socio-economic status.

Oral health behaviours of Vietnamese people were also a focus of the survey and raised a number of areas of concern. It was identified that prevention education and general dental hygiene practices were key areas requiring attention for improvements to be realised. The behavioural survey results are listed in Table 2.4. Note that different questions were provided for children and adults.

Table 2.4 Outcomes of the second national survey of oral health of Viet Nam [31]

Behaviour	Children	Adult
Brushed teeth yesterday	94.2	90.9
Brushing frequency		
1 time on average	N/A	40.6
2+ times/day on average	52.6	51.3
Started using toothpaste		
Under 5 years of age	34.2	N/A
5+ years	39.7	N/A
Don't know	26.0	N/A
Used toothpaste yesterday	N/A	90.8
Last dental visit		
Never visited for dental care	10.4	55.0
More than 2 years ago	67.3	15.9
Last 2 years	22.3	29.1
Prevalence of permanent dental caries	53.2	95.0

The reasons for poor oral health are seen as manyfold. The key factors include:

- Negligible preventative care – most visits (66 %) to the dentist were for extractions or prescriptions to treat existing dental issues. Only 7 % of visits included a clean and scale procedure.
- Low level of oral hygiene practices.
- Late commencement of brushing.
- Smoking prevalence – over 35 % of the adult population smokes or has smoked regularly.
- Growth in westernised diet especially foods with high sugar content.
- Low access to dentists – the number of dentists per 100,000 population is 3.7 compared to 12 in Thailand, 76 in Japan, 7.5 in Indonesia and 49.5 in Australia. The number of dentists in Viet Nam is clearly significantly lower than in other Southeast Asian countries.

Recommendations:

- Comprehensive health and oral health programmes, taking into account the socio-economic aspect of oral health.
- Preventive orientation for the dental profession.
- Health and oral health education requires attention.
- Policy that understands the geographic and socio-economic disparities in dental health.

A number of these recommendations have subsequently been addressed either by other international groups or by the Vietnamese Government. There has been a focus in two areas: volunteer specialist teams providing access to dental surgery treatment in low-income areas and preventative education in schools across Viet Nam.

The Rotary Club of Australia has been especially active since 1992 with the first specialist team visiting in 1998 [30]. Most recently they have been involved in increasing capacity to manage cleft palate care in rural Viet Nam and since 2007 have been funding school-based preventative programmes and are providing voluntary dental health services including fillings and fissure sealing in the most disadvantaged areas.

The Vietnamese Government is implementing a range of policy-driven dental system improvements including: [31]

- A primary school-based oral health programme offered in eight provinces and cities across Viet Nam. The programme has three main activities:
  - Oral healthcare education
  - Provision of 0.2 % fluoride solution for children to rinse with weekly during school time
  - Clinical prevention through check-ups
- Water fluoridation trials in Ho Chi Minh City and Dong Nai
- A two-phase salt fluoridation project:
  - Phase 1 – a two-year pilot in Lao Cai Province (northern mountainous region)
  - Phase 2 – commenced in 2010 with planned future expansion to other provinces
- Student exchange with Australian universities to improve graduate and professional capacity.

These projects were recommended by, and received supplies and financial and human resources from, Adelaide and Melbourne Universities in Australia, the Viet Nam Outreach organisation and the WHO.

There are clearly advances being made in dental training and practice, especially in preventative programmes in Viet Nam, but this has all required international collaboration. There is increased local capacity being developed but many more quality graduates are required to meet the growing needs of the Vietnamese population and only time will tell if there is enough being done to meet and keep pace with demand in this field.

2.4.2.2 Psychology

Psychology is a recognised field of practice in Viet Nam; however, services are under-resourced both in terms of quality and quantity. There are reportedly only around 100 psychological counselling offices across the country with most being in Ho Chi Minh City [33, 34]. It is estimated that the number of practising psychologists only meets 5 % of the demand in Ho Chi Minh City alone [33]. The social ramification of this is that few know that psychological counselling is available or what it can offer to the individual or communities. A survey of 100 people in Hanoi in 2011 revealed that only 13 % of people know about the availability of psychological counselling services offices and 87 % did not have any knowledge on the topic [34]. Other research has identified that one barrier to the understanding of psychological counselling services in Viet Nam is that the word ‘counselling’ has no real equivalent in the Vietnamese language and the concept of consultation-based service is not understood. Patients expect to see a medical professional, receive a treatment and then go away until the next condition requiring attention develops [35]. These factors not only impact upon service demand but also on the attractiveness of psychology as a career path. It is estimated that only 20 % of graduates from psychology programmes enter practice as a result [33]. Naturally this creates one of the many vicious circles in Vietnamese healthcare.

There is a strong focus on psychology services for children as they have been most affected by the changes in the Vietnamese landscape. They are the first generation to have a disposable income, technology, mobility opportunities and a highly competitive education and career environment. Research has revealed that up to 90 % of school-age children suffer from some level of psychological difficulty which directly impacts on their learning and ability to cope on a daily basis [36, 37]. Approximately 20 % of children suffer from clinical depression, anxiety or oppositional defiant disorders [37]. This represents around seven million children that require some level of psychological support, hence the focus on school-level psychological service improvement. One of the biggest triggers in the development of psychological issues in children is the fear of failure. Almost 65 % of students are constantly afraid of receiving low grades, and this fear is both built and exacerbated by the fact that 97 % of parents openly report that they want their children to perform above average at school [38]. Given the cultural beliefs in Viet Nam as described earlier, children do not wish to disappoint their parents or teachers, but clearly 97 % of all children cannot be above average in a single class, and hence almost half do not achieve their own or their parents’ goals in education.

In an effort to address the evidence calling for improved mental health support for school-age children, the Ministry of Education and Training (MoET) issued two official directives to all schools (2564/BGD&DT-HSSV and 9971/BGD&DT-HSSV) [38]. These directives recommended the implementation of vocational and psychological counselling services for all children in each school. Whilst an important initiative, there was no funding available for implementation so again the focus turned to international collaborations to drive the work forwards.

The gap between supply and demand for psychological services was recognised by St. John’s University (STJ) in 2007 [35]. The education psychology school funded an exploratory visit to Hanoi to learn about the Vietnamese educational system and to develop a relationship with MoET professionals. Follow-up visits the following year established a formal collaboration with faculty from the Hanoi National University of Education to establish a school psychology training programme and conduct six 20-h training courses in a ‘train-the-trainer’ model.

At the same time as STJ was providing capacity building within Viet Nam, another collaboration was being built between the Institute of Psychology (IOP) in Viet Nam and the school psychology programme at California State University, Long Beach (CSULB) [36]. The success of the STJ and CSULB initiatives prompted the establishment of the Consortium to Advance School Psychology in Viet Nam (CASP-V) in 2010 [36]. The aim of the consortium was to further develop the relationship and collaborative opportunities between US and Vietnamese universities and develop a specialised school psychology training programme. The nature of these key collaborations has influenced the providers and focus of psychology programmes in Viet Nam.

Current psychology-teaching institutions [33, 36]:

- Faculty of Social Sciences and Humanities – Viet Nam National University, Hànôi
- Faculty of Social Sciences and Humanities – Viet Nam National University, Ho Chi Minh City
- Dong A University, Da Nang
- Faculty of Education – University of Da Nang
- Faculty of Education – Hue University
- Faculty of Educational Psychotherapy – Hanoi National University of Education
- Faculty of Military Psychotherapy, University of Politics
- The Department of Educational Psychotherapy at the Thái Nguyên University of Education
- Institute of Psychology (IOP)

Although there is a focus on programme content aimed at school counselling and guidance from international counterparts, the MoET directive discussed earlier did not specify the academic foundations, graduate outcomes or professional capabilities required to practise as a psychological counsellor in Viet Nam. As a result of this lack of direction or quality metrics, most universities do not have tailored training courses in general psychology. Most of those providing psychological services outside of schools are therefore graduates of programmes such as law, journalism or marketing and usually receive only short-term training prior to practising [33, 36]. This training is commonly only of 3 days' duration and is not by any means an in-depth study of psychology or counselling skills [33]. As stated earlier, psychology is not seen as a profession upon which to build a career, and hence providers do not consider it a long-term job. Many enter the job part time or as a stop gap until they secure permanent employment in their preferred field. Surveys reveal that counsellors have low confidence in their knowledge of evidence-based practices and limited understanding of available training and resources [36]. This lack of dedication to the field and access to capacity-building opportunities results in a very low willingness to invest in professional development to improve their skills or enhance their knowledge. This results in a professional stagnation and sustained call for service delivery improvement.

The lack of dedicated psychology programmes in universities impacts on the form of psychological services delivered at the grass-roots level. Most providers other than private western-staffed clinics work within a similar service model and offer advice through online forums, phone calls, SMS, voice mail, email and magazines [33, 36]. As mentioned earlier, the western notion of consultative counselling is not familiar, and hence most services are delivered through a nonpersonal medium or through focused workshops on such topics as life skills and communication skills in family and society. If a consultative approach is taken, practitioners do little more than listen to their clients' problems, offer sympathy for their situation and then offer advice based on personal experience [33]. This is hardly surprising given that most have had 3 days' training at best.

For the practice of psychology to move forwards, there must be a stronger direction forged by the MoST and the MOH; capacity building at the practice and academic level must be consolidated and enhanced; the population should be informed regarding the availability of services and the assistance that is provided; and the profession should be made more attractive to students and graduates. This will take a change of culture, a development of general psychology programmes with defined graduate outcomes, a professional capabilities framework, professional development opportunities and a significant time and financial investment by a range of stakeholders.

2.4.2.3 Physiotherapy

Physiotherapy is a seriously underdeveloped service in Viet Nam with only six clinics listed for the country of which four are foreign run and staffed [39, 40]. All foreign providers are in private practice and are thus out of reach for most Vietnamese. The two Vietnamese physiotherapy providers are within local hospitals and are by appointment only [40].

Development of the first formal training programme in physiotherapy is being facilitated through a recent memorandum of understanding between the Australian Dreamin Foundation, Inc., the Hue College of Medicine and Pharmacy and the Office of Genetic Counselling and Disabled Children in Hue. The aim is to develop a specialised programme of study in early rehabilitation and physiotherapy training. The project is jointly funded by the Dreamin Foundation, Inc., and Rotary Club of Prospect, Inc. [41]. This sponsorship extends to supporting regular visits by a paediatric physiotherapist who works with disadvantaged and disabled children in central Viet Nam. The specialist works with local practitioners and develops individual treatment programmes and orders and fits any equipment each child requires. This equipment includes wheelchairs, standing frames and special seating, etc. The whole community benefits as the equipment is procured through local companies which provides income and employment for many local tradespeople.

The impact of this initiative, although very localised, cannot be overstated. Through the personalised treatment programme and the prescribed equipment, children are able to transition from living in an immobilised state on the floor to being able to stand and walk. Many of the children were so badly affected that they could not sit up independently and spent their lives lying on their side [29]. Such children were provided with special seating and for the first time could join their classmates around a table and participate in play activities. Simply put, children that were previously excluded from normal childhood activities, experiences and education could lead a relatively normal life. The impact of this upon the individual, their family and their potential to become value-adding members of the community rather than a burden and drain on resources is immeasurable.

The desperate need for physiotherapy support in Viet Nam, mainly through accidents and birth defects, has caught the attention of a number of Australian and US universities and volunteer organisations [42–46]. The main focus is in providing professional development and mentoring opportunities for health professionals and to provide on ground capacity through a large number of volunteer initiatives. Unfortunately, due to the limited number of people available, current efforts are constrained to three locations, Ho Chi Minh City, Hanoi and Da Nang, and hence few have access to these essential services. Whilst the services that are delivered are providing measured benefit to recipients, it is not sustainable, and a dedicated effort driven through the ministries is required to develop and consolidate a body of practice supported by high-quality programmes of study both in physiotherapy and equipment engineering. Without the current level of engagement and funding from international groups, the practice of physiotherapy would cease to exist in Viet Nam.

2.5 Professional Training and Development

Viet Nam has a vibrant and growing education system at all levels from kindergarten to higher degrees. There is a defined strategic direction from the government to build capacity in Viet Nam and to encourage students to move into university study. Places are often very competitive with students and parents becoming consumed by the university entrance exam process. High school students have only one opportunity to gain a position in the best Vietnamese universities and many have anecdotally suffered from significant mental stresses both before and after the exam period with reports of suicide not uncommon if failure results.

Due to pay scales in Viet Nam for medical practitioners (average 150–200 USD a month base rate [2] or 15–22.5 k USD including all bonuses [47]), there is not the same attraction to medicine for students as seen in western countries where salaries are ten times higher [48]. Most parents prefer their children to undertake technology or business studies; however, there are still entrance exams and competition to secure the best students by non-medical schools. For example, 10,500 applicants competed for 800 seats at Hanoi Medical University in 2007 [2]. Generally only between 10 % and 40 % of applications are successful [49].

Whilst salaries are low, the fees for studying medicine in Viet Nam are also significantly lower than in western countries and across the board are less than 1000 USD per year. This is still a considerable investment in a country whose per capita income in 2014 is around 1730 USD per year [50] and where 500 USD per month is considered a high salary and puts the receiver in the 'rich' category [2].

Viet Nam has a three-tiered medical education system. In western countries these tiers usually exist within one institution. A university is composed of colleges and the colleges are further divided into schools. In Viet Nam these entities are often separate but with loose connections which allow Vietnamese medical students to progress through various levels of education, similar to the vocational and university pathways in other countries. However, there are also instances where all three types of entity reside within a single institution in Viet Nam presenting a very complex environment in which to offer, manage, monitor, review and accredit programmes of study.

The duration of an undergraduate medical degree in Viet Nam is 6 years which compares to most other medical programmes globally; however, there are three key differences. The first difference is that there is no comparable in service training component, no core rotations and no study electives. All students follow essentially the same programme structure and complete the same broad series of courses as defined by the MoET. Individual institutions are able to independently develop their own content, and there are no consistent national graduate outcomes or other quality measures upon which to compare programmes, readiness to practise or professional competency.

The second key difference is in the inclusion of physical education and political studies in all degrees in Viet Nam including medicine. English language studies is also a requirement in medical degrees. This consumes much of the first year of study. A sample programme structure and schedule is included in Appendix A.

The third difference that was described anecdotally is that whilst all medical graduates previously swore to uphold the Hippocratic Oath when graduating, since 2010 the government decreed that all must now swear allegiance to Ho Chi Minh and his teachings. Medical students and many faculty reportedly do not like this change and see it as an initiative that will further harm the perception of Vietnamese healthcare and medical school integrity around the world.

There is no specialisation until postgraduate study where students can choose a clinical or research pathway. Entry to postgraduate places is even more competitive than undergraduate with an exam and interview. To sit the entrance exam candidates must have passed all undergraduate courses with no failures and have achieved a GPA of at least seven out of ten [2]. Whilst entry requirements are high, postgraduate study is not attractive to doctors, and there are concerns within the government that the quality of healthcare services in Viet Nam is compromised. As a result there are plans to increase the attractiveness and enrolments in postgraduate programmes. One idea that has been floated in a 2015 conference is to reduce the entry requirements; however, this scenario is common in many programmes in western universities and has not demonstrated an ability to facilitate higher-quality outcomes, so caution is advised. There are intentions to develop a programme of continuing professional development for medical professionals, including nurses and pharmacists, but the structure, implementation and even framework of understanding of how this might look are yet to be defined. Another new initiative focused on licencing of medical practitioners has begun, and a requirement for some measure of continued professional development, as seen in other countries, for licence renewal is a possible inclusion.

All universities offer undergraduate and postgraduate programmes. Postgraduate programmes are 2 years' duration for masters or 3 years for PhD.

Although there is no formal accreditation of medical degrees as seen in western medical schools, there are a set of ministry guidelines, but these were not formalised until the mid-2000s, and most institutions are not yet implementing the standards [51]. Only three universities have adopted internal monitoring and self-accreditation against the ministry standards: Ho Chi Minh City University of Medicine and Pharmacy, Hanoi Medical University and Thai Nguyen University. All three have called for external monitoring and assessment of these standards to provide a level of independent validation of compliance and quality. There are moves to address the lack formalised accreditation through projects funded by the Asian Development Bank and the World Bank in 2015. Accreditation based upon the global standard developed by the World Federation for Medical Education is believed to be the intended strategic direction and will certainly enhance the global standing and local quality for Vietnamese healthcare if appropriately implemented and managed. There are however a number of issues in implementation. There are several highly invested persons who have developed localised standards and do not believe that international standards and accreditation processes are relevant to Viet Nam. There are also concerns that the Vietnamese essence of the medical programme including the requirement of political studies, etc., may be compromised if an international model is adopted and again there is resistance to this from both high-ranking ministry and university representatives. Finding common ground will not be easy. There are therefore barriers to overcome before accreditation that is recognised outside of Viet Nam is able to be implemented. There is support from the Minister for health for international standards to be followed, and hence progress is expected to occur inevitably, but significant work will be required to ensure there is agreement from all stakeholders on the way forwards. The development of a road map and agreed standards will require international experts as current work has been very inward facing to date hence the projects by the ADB and World Bank valued at well over 100 M USD. This work is expected to take up to 6 years and has been integrated into the 2020 vision for health.

There are 18 institutions including 10 universities offering medical-focused degrees in Viet Nam. The largest university is Hanoi Medical University. The following is an overview of university-level institutions in Viet Nam [49, 52–56] (Tables 2.5).

The following higher-degree specialisations are offered by each of the providers. Each university is denoted by its corresponding number in the table above (Table 2.6).

Whilst there are many universities and medical programmes available, it is interesting to note that none of these openly advertise the availability of continuing professional education. As discussed earlier this is a focus of new initiatives in Vietnamese medical education and will serve to ensure medical practitioners from all fields maintain currency of skills and knowledge. This is especially important in a country such as Viet Nam which has a changing health environment and an evolving policy and finance platform. One key omission that has been identified is a lack of management training at any level. This is true of many fields in Viet Nam, but it has a significant impact in the health domain as many of the planned initiatives require strong management to develop policy frameworks for governance and to project manage and evaluate outcomes and performance.

Table 2.5 Overview of medical universities (student numbers aggregated from several sources)

University	Description
Tay Nguyen University 567 Le Duan, Buon Ma Thuot, Dak Lak Province Phone: +84 50 382 5185 Fax: +84 50 283 5184 http://www.taynguyenuni.edu.vn/home/	Founded in 1977 Ranking in Viet Nam, 72 Population served, 1.5–2 m Teaching faculty, 102 Students, 3000
Can Tho University (CTU) 3/2 Street, Xuan Khanh Ward, Ninh Kieu District, 92000, Can Tho City Tel: +84 710 383 2663 Fax: +84 710 383 8474 http://www.ctu.edu.vn/index_e.htm	Founded in 1966 Ranking in Viet Nam, 3 Population served, 1–5 m Teaching faculty, 192 Students, 5000
Pham Ngoc Thach University of Medicine 86/2 Thanh Thai Q10, Ho Chi Minh City Tel: +84 88 650 021 Fax: +84 88 650 025 http://www.pnt.edu.vn	Founded in 1989 Ranking in Viet Nam, 77 Population served, >5 m Teaching faculty, 193 Students, 2000
Hai Phong Medical University 72A, Street Nguyen Binh, Khiem District, Hai Phong Tel: +84 31 847 907 Fax: +84 31 852 224 http://hpmu.edu.vn/yhaiphong/vn/home/index.jsp	Founded in 1979 Ranking in Viet Nam, 56 Population served, 1–5 m Teaching faculty, 200–300 Students, 3000
Thai Binh Medical University 373 LyBon Street, Thai Binh City, Thai Binh, 33000 Tel: +84 36 838 545 Fax: +84 36 847 509 http://www.tbmc.edu.vn/	Founded in 1968 Ranking in Viet Nam, 19 Population served, 1.5–2 m Teaching faculty, 200–300 Students, 4500
Hanoi Medical University 1 Ton That Tung Street, Dong Da District, Hanoi 10000 Tel: +84 48 523 798 Fax: +84 48 525 115 http://www.hmu.edu.vn/TiengAnh/	Founded in 1902 Ranking in Viet Nam, 15 Population served, >5 m Teaching faculty, 1000–1500 Students, 6000–7000

(continued)

Table 2.5 (continued)

University	Description
Huê University 3, Lê Loi, Hue 43100 Tel: +84 54 823 749 http://hueuni.edu.vn/portal/index.php	Founded in 1957 Ranking in Viet Nam, 10 Population served, <0.5 m Teaching faculty, 1500–2000 Students, 7750
Thai Nguyên University Km 4, Duong 14, Tan Thinh Ward, Thai Nguyen Tel: +84 280 385 2650 Fax: +84 280 385 2665 http://www.taynguyenuni.edu.vn/home	Founded in 1994 Ranking in Viet Nam, 33 Population served, 0.25 m Teaching faculty, 3000–3500 Students, 4200
Ho Chi Minh City University of Medicine and Pharmacy 217 Hong Bang, Quang 5, Ho Chi Minh City 15000 Tel: +84 8 558 411 Fax: +84 8 552 304 http://moodle.yds.edu.vn/yds2	Founded in 1947 Ranking in Viet Nam, 13 Population served, >5 m Teaching faculty, 230 Students, 4500
Viet Nam Military Medical University Phung Hung Street, Ha Dong District, Hanoi Tel: +84 693 566 100 www.hocvienquany.vn	Founded in 1966 Ranking in Viet Nam, N/A Population served, >5 m Teaching faculty, N/A Students, 4000

The following is a representative undergraduate medical programme description from Tay Nguyen University (also known as the University of Western Highlands) as decreed by the 'Ministry of Education and Training of the Socialist Republic of Viet Nam, issued in Decision No. 992/QD-DDTHTN-DTDH, August 17, 2009' [57].

1 Training Objectives:

1.1 General Objectives

Training doctors will gain knowledge of general medical ethics, basic science, hospital administration and operations, basic skills of clinical medicine and community. The programme combines modern medicine with traditional medicine and enables graduates to meet the need for care and protection of people's health.

1.2. Specific Objectives

1.2.1. Knowledge

Table 2.6 Medical specialisation programmes

University #	1	2	3	4	5	6	7	8	9	10
Specialties offered										
Allergology and immunology				X						
Anaesthesia/resuscitation		X							X	X
Anatomopathology and legal medicine				X						
Anatomy		X		X						X
Biochemistry		X								X
Biology and heredity				X						
Chemistry and biochemistry				X						
Clinical medicine			X							
Community health			X							
Dentistry										X
Dento-Maxilo-Faciological							X			
Dermatology		X		X					X	X
Diagnostic imaging									X	X
Ear, nose and throat				X						X
Endocrinology									X	
Environmental health					X					
Epidemiology					X					X
Family medicine		X								
General internal medicine	X									
General medicine							X			
Gerontology									X	
Haematology		X							X	X
Histo-embryology		X								
Histology and fetology				X						
Imaging diagnosis										
Immunology										X
Infectious diseases	X	X		X						X
Informatics				X						
Internal medicine		X		X						X
Marine medicine				X						
Maxilo-Odontology						X				
Medical ethics									X	
Medical Technology										
Mental health			X				X			
Microbiology										X
Neurology		X		X					X	
Nuclear Medicine				X					X	
Nursing									X	X
Obstetric and gynaecology	X	X		X			X		X	
Odonto-Maxillo-Fasciology		X		X						
Oncology		X		X					X	

(continued)

Table 2.6 (continued)

University #	1	2	3	4	5	6	7	8	9	10
Ophthalmology	X			X						
Orthopaedics		X							X	X
Otolaryngology		X		X					X	X
Otonasolaryngology									X	
Paediatrics		X						X	X	
Parasitology – entomology	X	X		X					X	X
Paratology	X									
Pathology				X						
Pathophysiology, pharmacology		X								X
Pharmacy				X					X	X
Physiology				X	X			X		
Physiotherapy-rehabilitation		X		X						X
Preventive medicine										
Psychiatry								X		
Psychology		X					X		X	
Public health		X			X	X		X		X
Radiology and imagery diagnosis				X			X			
Rehabilitation	X			X						
Sports medicine		X								
Surgery										X
Tuberculosis									X	X
Traditional medicine	X	X		X						
Underwater medicine			X				X			X
Urology										X

Develop an understanding of the basic rules of medical practice:

- The anatomy, operation and function of the human body in normal and pathological scenarios
- The interaction between the environment and human health and measures to maintain and improve living conditions to protect and improve health
- The basic principles of diagnosis and prevention
- The law and policy of the state to care to protect and improve people's health
- Scientific methodology appropriate for prevention, treatment and scientific research

1.2.2. Skills

- Provision of medical consultations, education, organisation of care and improving people's health.
- Propose appropriate measures to the Vietnamese context to improve public and environmental health.
- Diagnosis and management of common diseases and some common emergencies.

- Diagnostic competency as a disease specialist.
- Specify and evaluate a number of appropriate technical testing and probing services for the diagnosis of common diseases.
- Undertake early detection of workplace hazards.
- Propose and implement appropriate prevention programmes.
- Apply traditional medicine in prevention and healing.
- Use at least one foreign language to read and understand literature.

1.2.3. Attitude

- Be devoted to the cause of caring, protecting and improving people's health and wholeheartedly serve patients.
- Show respect for, and cooperate with, colleagues.
- Know, preserve and promote the traditions of the industry.
- Always be modest and engage in continued study.

1.2.4. Ability to Practise

- After graduation, the doctor has the ability to work in a medical setting and practise as a general doctor at the central, provincial, district and community level.

2 Duration of training: 6 year

- Medical knowledge courses: 208 credits
- General education knowledge: 42 credits
- Physical education: 3 credits
- National defence education reference: 7 credits
- Theory of Marx-Lenin and Ho Chi Minh Thought: 10 credits
- Social sciences: 2 credits
- Foreign language: 7 credits
- Mathematics and natural sciences: 23 credits

3 Vocational education knowledge: 156 credits, composed of:

- Knowledge base sector: 60 credits
- Knowledge of industry: 86 credits
- Graduation thesis (or professional module replacement): 10 credits

4 Enrolment group: students graduating from high school or equivalent.

5 Graduation requirements: graduates must meet the 'Academic Regulation Training requirements for the formal college credit system', issued through Decision No. 742/QD-TNU-DTDH dated June 8, 2009, by the Rector of the University of Highlands, and the 'Regulation Training university and college system of government credit system' issued through Decision No. 43/2007/QD-BGDDT dated August 15, 2007, by the Ministry of Education and Training.

These guidelines and requirements are audited by the ministry, and hence documentation demonstrating compliance and constant improvement must be provided as demonstrated in the following example for Tay Nguyen University [57].

Library

The School Information and Literacy Centre and the State Library have received a huge investment. The total area of the centre is nearly 3000 m^2. The library centre has Internet access and a networked information e-library.

Curriculum and Training Lectures

The number of textbooks and e-books in the library is updated annually. Library resources include textbooks, reference books and other training programme materials to meet the academic requirements of research staff, faculty and students.

Implementation of the Programme

The general practitioner training is based on the framework programme by the Ministry of Education and Training and the Ministry of Health requirements and includes training on specific diseases in the central highland regions.

Programme completion requires 208 core credits of medical education.

Teaching Practice

Knowledge and practice of general education shall comply with the regulations of the Ministry of Education and Training. Teaching methods include presentation methods, questioning and combining theory with practice.

Application of Professional Education

Internship: practical teaching is conducted in a laboratory according to the regulations of the Ministry of Education and Training and the Ministry of Health. Laboratory practice learning is a component of the theory test. Each internship is 2 weeks' long.

Community: there will be two fieldwork sessions of 2 weeks' duration each in the community scheduled as follows:

- Session 1: at the end of the third year after completion of the course covering basic medical, preclinical medicine, education and improving health organisations
- Session 2: at the end of the fifth year after the student has completed the epidemiology component and most subjects in clinical medicine

Methods of Teaching/Learning

Students self-study through exposure to visual media and active teaching and learning methods. The university ensures textbooks and reference materials are available for students. As the programme progresses, a reduction of class hours in theory is encouraged as is an increase in self-study opportunities for students.

Assessment

Testing is conducted after each module to accumulate credits and evaluate knowledge gained.

- For basic sciences, medicine and preclinical courses, after each module students must gain a theory test score.
- For clinical medicine, after each module students must gain scores through both theory and practical examination.

Scoring

Scoring of assessment must follow the guidelines as stated in the regulations on the training, testing, implementation and recognition of graduation approvals from the university and college system as regulated by Decision No. 43/2007/QD-BGDDT dated August 15, 2007, from the Ministry of Education and Training [57].

Given the range of courses taught as part of the medical programme, it is self-evident that a broad range of teaching specialisations are also required. Unlike most western medical faculties, Viet Nam includes foreign language, politics and physical education staff. Most of these staff have lower qualifications than those teaching pure sciences or clinical courses. Data across 3 universities revealed that on average 43.5 % of medical school faculty have a bachelor's degree as the highest degree, 38.7 % have a masters degree and 17.8 % have a PhD [29, 51, 57]. Clinical courses were all taught by masters or PhD holders.

2.6 Trends in the Vietnamese Healthcare Landscape

As stated in the introduction, the Vietnamese healthcare landscape is changing rapidly. There is an aging population and new public health issues are emerging as a result of greater affluence and exposure to western diets and stress. The general trend has been away from communicable diseases and towards chronic non-communicable diagnoses [1]. In 1976, 55.5 % of all diagnoses were for communicable diseases. By 2008 this figure had reduced to 25.2 %. Over the same period, non-communicable diagnoses have increased by 20 %, whilst injuries, accidents and poisoning-related conditions remained relatively stable at around 10 %.

The total disease burden in 2008 was measured at 12.3 million disability-adjusted life years (DALYs) with non-communicable disease being responsible for 71 % of that figure [58]. Cardiovascular disease was the leading cause of burden for adults followed by stroke and depression and pneumonia headed the list forchildren [58]. Table 2.7 shows the baseline and projections against the current Ministry of Health defined indicators.

The changes in disease burden from communicable to non-communicable presents a dramatic shift in the knowledge base required for effective practice by medical professionals. It also calls for education programmes in the general population to ensure that sufferers know where, how and when to seek treatment as there is not a community knowledge base to call upon, and if practitioners are also not fully informed, then a scenario where disease becomes endemic and chronic develops and places an unnecessary strain on individuals, families and community resources.

Table 2.7 Health indicators and projected improvements to 2015 [59]

No.	Indicator	2010	Estimate 2015
1	Life expectancy at birth (years)	73.0	74
2	Size of population (million inhabitants)	86,920	<92
3	Population growth rate reduction (%)	0.2	0.2
4	Population growth rate (%)	1.04	0.94
5	Sex ratio at birth (boys/100 girls)	111	113
6	Hospital bed per 10,000 inhabitants (exclude CHS bed)	20.5	23.0
7	Number of doctors/10,000 inhabitants	7	8
8	Number of pharmacists/10,000 inhabitants	1.2	1.8
9	Villages with active VHW	85	90
10	Commune with doctor (%)	70	80
11	Commune with midwife (%)	>95	>95
12	% of commune achieving new national health benchmark	N/A	60
13	Health insurance coverage (%)	60	80
14	Fully vaccinated infants (%)	>90	>90
15	HIV/AIDS prevalence (%)	<0.3	<0.3
16	Under-five child malnutrition rate (weight for age) (%)	18.0	15.0
17	MMR (p100,000)	68	58.3
18	IMR (p1000) <16 14	<16	14
19	Under-five mortality rate (p1000)	25	19.3

Unfortunately there is little evidence to suggest this knowledge shift has occurred or that medical training has kept pace with the changing needs of the population.

References

1. U.S. Government Global Health Initiative Strategy (2011) Vietnam V5.0. Aug 2011
2. Tran H, Pretorius R (2008) Vietnamese [sic] medical education and development of family medicine in Vietnam. State University of New York at Buffalo School of Medicine and Biomedical Sciences. VMGUS Publication No 052009
3. VietNam News (2012) Pediatric hospitals overcrowded. March 14 2012. http://vietnamnews.vn/society/222113/pediatric-hospitals-overcrowded.html. Accessed 12 Oct 2014
4. Tran BX, Minh HV, Hinh ND (2013) Factors associated with job satisfaction among commune health workers: implications for human resource policies. Global Health Action 6. doi:10.3402/gha.v6i0.18619
5. Shillabeer A (2013) Development of an E-health strategic framework for Vietnam. Chapter 19, pp 163–173. In: Proceedings of the international conference on managing the Asian century: ICMAC 2013. In: Mandal P (ed) Springer Science & Business Media, 2014. ISBN 9814560618, 9789814560610. 668 Pages
6. Nguyen VT, Ha D A, Tran MO, Prakongsai P, Tangcharoensathien V (2011) The independent assessment of the process and the content of the five year health plan, 2011–15, in Vietnam. Final report 7 Jan 2011. Ministry of Health of Viet Nam, Health Partnerships Group, Joint Ann Health Rev 2011. Hanoi

7. World Health Organization (2008) World health statistics 2008. ISBN 978 92 4 156359 8 (NLM classification: WA 900.1) ISBN 978 92 4 0682740 (electronic version)
8. Khuu DT (1999) Vietnamese health care. World Health Care. Stanf Med Rev. 1:1
9. Tran H, BSc Hon, Pretorius R (2009) Vietnamese medical education and development of family medicine in Vietnam. VMGUS Publication No 052009. http://www.vietmd.net/VMGUS_VN_FMResidency1.pdf. Accessed 14 Jan 2015
10. www.cancerindex.org/Vietnam. Last updated 06 Dec 2014. Accessed 4 Jan 2015
11. Palliative Care Australia (2003) Palliative care service provision in Australia: A Planning Guide. www.palliativecare.org.au/Portals/46/Palliative%20Care%20Service%20Provision%20in%20Australia%20-%20a%20planning%20guide.pdf. Accessed 6 Jan 2015
12. Hoefler JM (2012) Palliative care at the end of life in western Europe: the Scandinavian paradox. In: Steffan L, Hinerman N (eds) New perspectives on the end of life: essays on care and the intimacy of dying. Inter-Disciplinary Press, Oxford. ISBN 9781848880979
13. Irish Cancer Society. www.cancer.ie/about-us/media-centre/cancer-statistics#sthash.ON4scOn4.dpbs. Accessed 6 Dec 2014
14. Murray E (2013) Access to specialist palliative care services and place of death in Ireland. May 2013. www.hospicefoundation.ie/wp-content/uploads/2013/06/Access-to-specialist-palliative-care-services-place-of-death-in-Ireland.pdf. Accessed 6 Jan 2015
15. Viet Nam Australia Family Health Service. Personal conversation with the clinic director Dr. Ron van Konkelenberg in Hanoi. January 2015
16. Nghiem DT (2010) Social health insurance in Viet Nam. Health Insurance Dept, Ministry of Health. Ha Noi, 12 Oct 2010. http://www.ilo.org/wcmsp5/groups/public/---asia/---ro-bangkok/---ilo-hanoi/documents/presentation/wcms_145792.pdf. Accessed 10 Nov 2014
17. World Life Expectancy (2014) http://www.worldlifeexpectancy.com/world-rankings-total-deaths. Accessed 12 Nov 2014
18. Central Intelligence Agency (CIA) (2012) East & southeast Asia: Vietnam. https://www.cia.gov/library/publications/the-world-factbook/geos/vm.html. Accessed 7 Feb 2014
19. World Health Organisation (2013) Global health observatory. Total expenditure on health as a percentage of gross domestic product (US$). http://www.who.int/gho/health_financing/total_expenditure/en/. Accessed 12 Nov 2014
20. Kaiser Family Foundation (2014) Global health facts. Physicians (Per 10,000 Population) http://kff.org/global-indicator/physicians/. Accessed 12 Nov 2014
21. WHO, UNICEF, UNFPA, The World Bank and the United Nations Population Division estimates (2014) Trends in maternal mortality 1990 to 2013. ISBN 978 92 4 150722 6. http://apps.who.int/iris/bitstream/10665/112682/2/9789241507226_eng.pdf. Accessed 14 Jan 2015
22. Vuong QA, Nguyen CT (2011) Vietnam Hai Thuong Lan Ong Y structure and ethnic medicine. Institute of Vietnamese Studies. www.vietsciences.free.fr/vietnam/vanhoa/savants/haithuonglanong.htm. Accessed 6 Dec 2014
23. vi.wikipedia.org/wiki/H%E1%BA%A3i_Th%C6%B0%E1%BB%A3ng_L%C3%A3n_%C3%94ng. Accessed 4 Oct 2014
24. Vietnamese Family Health. Health beliefs and healing practices www.vietfamilyhealth.org/culture/beliefs.html. Accessed 12 Jan 2015
25. Lugmayr L (2013) Cupping craze spreads among Hollywood stars.1 http://www.celebrity-balla.com/2013/04/84605/cupping-craze-spreads-among-hollywood-stars#UIXTiifyhaz5t3PK.99. Accessed 12 Jan 2015
26. Yin Yang House (2006) Auricular acupuncture chart. http://www.yinyanghouse.com/theory/auricular/acupuncture_chart. Accessed 12 Jan 2015
27. Nghiem Minh Association (2014) Mobile mental health support in Vietnam. January, 2014. www.slideshare.net/loctran/mobile-mental-health-support-in-vietnam. Accessed 21 Aug 2014
28. Viet Nam Military University Hospital. www.hocvienquany.vn/. Accessed 3 Oct 2014
29. Thai Nguyen University. http://vi.wikipedia.org/wiki/Tr%C6%B0%E1%BB%9Dng_%C4%90%E1%BA%A1i_h%E1%BB%. Accessed 3 Oct 2014

30. Libit H (1997). In Hanoi, operation smile dentists: university of Maryland dental students and teachers are taking their skills to the children of Vietnam for two weeks. The Baltimore Sun. 28 Dec 1997. http://articles.baltimoresun.com/1997-12-28/news/1997362062_1_maryland-dental-school-dental-care-hanoi. Accessed 30 Oct 2014
31. Vietnam – Australian Oral Health Collaborative Initiatives (2010) Symposium on Vietnam-Australian Oral Health Initiatives 2010. www.oralhealthcrc.org.au/.../100514 VA symposium release.pdf. Accessed 10 Nov 2014
32. University of British Columbia (2012) UBC Dentistry opens oral health research centre in Vietnam. 31 Dec 2012. www.dentistry.ubc.ca/ubc-dentistry-opens-oral-health-research-centre-in-vietnam/. Accessed 30 Oct 2014
33. Pham DD (2012) Psychological counselling services in social mental and healthcare in Vietnam today. Soc Sci Inf Rev 6(2), June 2012
34. Nguyễn T, Hoàng M (2009) Hoang Nhan psychological counselling center. Broadcast on O2TV Channel. http://o2tv.vn. Accessed 16 Sept 2014
35. Terjesen MD, Kassay KS, Bolger M (2008) Developing the profession of school psychology in Vietnam. Communique 37(2):1, 8–11
36. Le P, Hagans K, Powers K, Hass M (2011) Developing school psychology in Vietnam. NASP. www.nasponline.org/publications/cq/39/6/SP-Vietnam.aspx. Accessed 5 Jan 2015
37. Nguyen AH, Le TMH, Tran PD (2007) Social, emotional, and behavioral difficulties among secondary school students. In: Dang BL, Bahr W (eds) Education, psychology, and mental health problems of Vietnamese children: theoretical and applied interdisciplinary research. Vietnam National University, Hanoi, pp 187–196
38. Ministry of Education and Training (2005) Develop counseling services for pupils and students. (9971/BGD&ĐT-HSSV). http://vanban.moet.gov.vn/?page=1.15&script=viewdoc&view=10463&opt=brpage. Accessed 14 Sept 2014
39. Family Medical Practice. www.vietnammedicalpractice.com/en/our-medical-services/physiotherapy/ho-chi-minh-city/ Office in Hanoi, Danang and HCMC. Accessed 13 Nov 2014
40. What Clinic. www.whatclinic.com/physiotherapy. Accessed 6 Jan 2014
41. Dreamin Foundation (2013) www.dreamin.org.au/projects/foundation-projects/project-vietnam. Accessed 22 Dec 2014
42. GoAbroad. www.goabroad.com/providers/projects-abroad/programs/physical-therapy-internships-in-vietnam-with-projects-abroad-92565. Accessed 10 Dec 2014
43. Sydney University. sydney.edu.au/health-sciences/community/partnerships /vietnam.shtml. Accessed 21 Dec 2014
44. GGC Volunteers. www.ggcvolunteers.org/#!children-support-vietnam/c132b. Accessed 21 Dec 2014
45. Charles Sturt University. www.csu.edu.au/csuglobal/short-term-programs/science/cmhealth/vietnam. Accessed 21 Dec 2014
46. Health Volunteers Overseas. https://hvousa.org/ourwork/programs/physical-therapy. Accessed 21 Dec 2014
47. Walters R (2014) Global salary survey. pp 463–470. www.robertwalters.com.au/wwwmedialibrary/WWW2/country/australia/content/salary-survey/robert-walters-2014-global-salary-survey.pdf. Accessed 10 Nov 2014
48. Japsen B (2013) Doctor pay rises to $221K for primary care, $396K for specialists. 6 Dec 2013. http://www.forbes.com/sites/brucejapsen/2013/06/12/doctor-pay-rises-to-221k-for-primary-care-396k-for-specialists/. Accessed 10 Jul 2014
49. www.4icu.org/reviews/12237.htm. Accessed 26 Oct 2014
50. World Bank (2013) http://data.worldbank.org/country/vietnam. Accessed 20 Nov 2014
51. Can Tho University. www.ctu.edu.vn/index_e.htm. Accessed 6 Jan 2015
52. www.classbase.com/countries/Vietnam/Universities. Accessed 13 Oct 2014
53. vietmd.net/forum/index.php?topic=554.5;wap2. Accessed 3 Oct 2014
54. Thai Nguyen University. www.ttn.edu.vn/tnu/index.php/en/2013-04-24-07-56-15/faculty-of-medicine-and-pharmacy. Accessed 12 Oct 2014

55. http://portal.ctump.edu.vn/en/index.php?option=com_content&view=article&id=531:departments&catid=208:faculty-of-medicine-&Itemid=235. Accessed 13 Oct 2014
56. www.uphcm.edu.vn/employee.aspx. Accessed 13th Oct 2014
57. www.taynguyenuni.edu.vn/home/html/307.htm. Accessed 24th Oct 2014
58. Nguyen NTT, Tran LK, Bui LN, Theo V, Nguyen HT, Ngo AD (2008) Estimation of Vietnam national burden of disease 2008. Asia Pac J Publ Health 26:527. doi:10.117/1010539513510556
59. Nguyen TKT, Pham TL, Nguyen LH, Pham TT, Bales S (eds) (2012) Joint Annual Health Review. Vietnamese Ministry of Health and Health Partnerships Group, Hanoi

Chapter 3
Culture and Belief Systems

The impact of culture can be viewed from three different perspectives. The first is from the perspective of training programmes which have some features that would not be seen in western medical programmes; the second is from the practice and patient participation aspect; and the third is from the perspective of workplace culture and the impact on human resources. Each of these will be looked at separately.

3.1 Culture and Training

All Vietnamese universities are required to incorporate politics teaching into every programme, and medical programmes are no exception. A second language is also required in medical programmes and is targeted towards continued learning after graduation through conferences and journals; however, few doctors maintain or develop their language skills, and poor communications may be a contributing factor in the perception that Viet Nam has poor medical support for foreigners.

It is believed that the origins of the now Vietnamese population are 5000 years old [1]. Whilst there have been significant Chinese, French and more recently American influences on the population, the core traditions have remained. There is still a deep faith in traditional health practices, and these remain a central focus for medical degrees in Viet Nam. Medical students learn how to select natural therapies and medications and how to administer traditional therapies.

So strong is the tradition that western practices can be misunderstood and poorly complied with by Vietnamese. For example, there is a belief that if symptoms subside, then they are cured and can discontinue medication or other treatments. This too often results in relapse or secondary issues especially in the case of infection treated by antibiotics which should be continued for some time after the obvious signs of infection have gone or subsided. Cancer is another example where the removal of the tumour can suggest the end of the disease, and hence completion of

A.G. Shillabeer, *The Health of Vietnam*, DOI 10.1007/978-981-287-709-3_3

radiotherapy and chemotherapy protocols is frequently lower in Viet Nam than in western countries.

Professional culture also has an impact on the provision or perceived provision of healthcare in Viet Nam. There are a number of newspaper reports detailing abhorrent practice caused by poor professional ethics. Poor patients often queue in hospital waiting rooms for hours only to see 'rich' patients offer money and receive immediate treatment, but they rarely complain openly [2]. In 2011, the Minister for health, Nguyen Thi Kim Tien, stated that 'unsympathetic behaviour of health workers, and taking black tips from patients is the biggest problem of the health sector'; however, the practice reportedly continues unabated [2].

There is also a belief that some doctors receive 'under the table' payments from pharmaceutical companies and overprescribe or prescribe more expensive medications for their patients than is necessary. Patients ask, 'Why doctors do not note the original names of medicines but the commercial names?' [2]. This would enable them to find alternative but equal medications for lower prices. Many cannot afford the prescribed medications and often turn to traditional and less effective or no treatments. A similar issue exists regarding medical tests with many patients not being able to afford the tests and hence going undiagnosed and therefore receiving suboptimal treatment in some cases which further exacerbates the perception that they receive poorer healthcare than those who have money. Nothing in Viet Nam is ever as simple as it seems!

Although this was clearly identified as a critical issue in healthcare by the Minister in 2011 even in 2014, atrocities are still occurring including the dumping of a dead body in a river to hide a bad surgery [3] and allegations of unlicenced practitioners being used to perform surgeries which resulted in the deaths of three children [4].

The unfortunate consequence of these stories is twofold. Firstly, there is an increasing loss of credibility across the medical profession, and patients no longer trust local doctors and services [5]. In the past 2 years, 14 doctors have been assaulted in hospitals by disenfranchised patients or their families [6]. The number of attacks could be much higher in fact as there are no official reports of how many incidents have actually occurred. Secondly, Vietnamese with high incomes are seeking medical treatment overseas especially Singapore, Korea and Thailand where treatment is considered higher quality and the problems of overcrowding seen in Viet Nam are not evident. It is estimated that health tourism from Viet Nam is worth over one billion USD and growing [7].

3.2 Cultural Influence on Practice and Patient Participation

Nationwide Strategy for the Vietnamese Family 2006–2010 states:

> Family is the cell of society where the human race is maintained, and which is an essential environment where human dignity is formed, taught and maintained; where good traditional culture is preserved and promoted; where social evils are warned against; and where

> human resources are supplied for nation-wide construction and defence...Family is one of the important factors determining the solid development of society, the success of industrialization and modernization and the building of Socialism. (p. 6)

Confucianism is a core part of Vietnamese cultural beliefs and has many pillars, one of the more relevant to this discussion is around the concept that greater suffering in this life means less suffering in the next [8]. The impact of this is that many Vietnamese do not feel compelled to seek medical assistance as early as would occur in the west. Confucianism also has two other important aspects that can affect health-seeking behaviours. These aspects are the collectivist family-orientated decision-making process and total respect for those in authority, including doctors [9]. The outcome of this is a disempowerment of the individual patient who believes that they have little more than a compliance part to play in their healthcare process and treatment option selection. This disempowerment is further exacerbated by an inability to question authority. Vietnamese patients are generally uncomfortable asking for a second opinion or if there are alternative treatments, and if their doctor does not tell them something, then they feel that there is nothing for them to know. They do not ask questions as this would suggest that the doctor has been negligible in fulfilling their needs and this is not a culturally acceptable attitude and may in fact influence or be perceived to influence their treatment from then on. This belief that doctors are experts leads to the expectation that they will be able to diagnose quickly and accurately; however, the process of diagnosis is complex and requires accurate inputs to produce accurate outputs from a consultation. This requirement for quality inputs is made more challenging in Viet Nam as there is a social norm of excessive politeness and a lack of acceptance for the practice of displaying open emotions. The Vietnamese will commonly hide their true feelings or fears as they do not wish to 'lose face' in their social group [1]. Hence, this further complicates any health consultation where there are few questions asked and an unwillingness to truthfully report pain, fear or anxiety. The doctor is working against the odds to fully understand a patient's true presentation and therefore cannot be expected to be able to provide a fast and accurate diagnosis. Some conditions such as mental health issues in particular are considered shameful and can further enhance the patient's need to hide the truth. Mental health issues are believed to be a punishment for sins in a past life, and a diagnosis casts a negative light on the family who are seen as tainted. Sometimes the whole community is so labelled, and the sufferer is often expelled to an uncertain and lonely existence to rid the family or social group of the curse. Mental illness is rarely discussed and remains a hidden problem with little community support or effective hospital services to assist [10]. Given the stigma, it would be social suicide for a person to describe symptoms of mental illness to a doctor and would instead present with other symptoms, such as headache, in the hope that any treatment would be a cure-all if it targets the affected area.

There is little evidence of a care industry in Viet Nam, and the family, especially the eldest son and his wife if he has one, is expected to provide a primary carer for the sick and elderly [1]. Elders teach younger members of the family or community about health matters, and this reduces the demand for support services such as antenatal or postnatal classes or disability assistance. Unfortunately, this can result in stagnation of knowledge and a lack of services in areas of growing demand such as child disability support [11]. For change to occur and enable improved outcomes, knowledge must evolve and incorporate current best practice; however, in Viet Nam, the traditional ways dominate, and few elders read medical literature or have the skills or finances to access information on the Internet or through other similar sources. This leads to a static state of community knowledge which is especially dangerous in a changing environment such as that in Viet Nam where new diagnoses are being encountered in increasing numbers. Many of these diagnoses have no traditional foundation upon which to apply existing knowledge and hence go untreated or poorly managed, and this increases the burden on the family and health systems. Whilst the negative impact of health illiteracy is growing, health education structures and mechanisms are not.

The lack of knowledge development and health literacy impacts significantly on the ability to introduce world standard treatment and diagnostic techniques to Viet Nam. Even routine blood tests are resisted wherever possible as the taking of blood is considered to create an imbalance in the body's Am and Duong or yin and yang in some other Asian cultures [12]. The belief that if there are no symptoms there is no illness presents a similar barrier to the introduction of preventative health measures, and this field of learning is currently outside of medical training programmes. Such practitioners are not considered doctors at all in fact.

The provision of timely, age-appropriate and culturally aware information is well documented to be key to a patient's experience in the healthcare system and a clinician's ability to provide best practice care. There are many benefits to be realised including:

- Greater compliance to treatment and recovery programmes
- Closer relationships and trust between patients and clinicians
- Lowered levels of depression and other mental problems
- Reduced fear and improved ability to cope with the stress of serious illness
- Reduced avoidable side effects
- Increased positive perception of the hospital and the clinical experience
- A greater ability to participate in decision-making regarding treatment options

This lack of information provision presents an almost intractable problem that stagnates any opportunity for progress at the population level and creates a situation where there is a growing gap between the need for outcome improvement and the ability to work within the cultural structures for personal health management.

3.3 Workplace Culture

Workplace maturity is relatively low in Viet Nam. There is a changing landscape triggered by an influx of western and outsourcing companies, especially in the technology industry, but within the healthcare sector, this has not yet presented a sufficient impetus for change. Professionals have generally trained, entered the workforce and then gathered skills and experience on the job and moved up the career ladder through internal promotion processes. There has been minimal professional development either demanded or provided and there has been little need. With a specialised skills shortage and heavily constrained budgets, healthcare organisations can simply not afford to provide ongoing training opportunities or function effectively without key staff for any length of time. Professional and administration staff are also unfamiliar with the concept of professional development, and with few programmes advertised, anecdotal evidence suggests they are not even aware that such opportunities exist beyond the highly competitive medical higher-degree programmes as discussed previously.

Whilst the overall number of human resources in health has grown significantly in recent decades, ensuring initial and ongoing quality of those resources remains a challenge for the sector. The focus is on providing resources for the public hospital sector, and there is little focus on emerging trends in healthcare resource needs and skills or on providing additional capacity especially in midwifery, paediatrics, public and preventative health and primary health settings [13]. Most alarming are reports from the Ministry of Health that the ratio of nurses to doctors is 1:3, and whilst only 27 % of the population lives in urban areas, 59 % of qualified doctors practice in these areas [13]. The government does understand the gaps and is developing programmes and expanding investment to address these and other defined target areas; however, it will take time for measurable change to be felt.

Health workers have come to expect that working conditions, resources and pay will be poor, especially in rural areas, and whilst many are unhappy, they are culturally dissuaded from complaining or making demands, and hence they are not the same drivers for change as seen in western countries. This presents a complex environment in which to identify foundations for change and implement and manage change effectively. Simply providing greater access to training, improving funding and developing new policies and national reform strategies are not sufficient. The track record of failure to effect national health improvement programmes is evidence of the resistance and/or lack of buy-in and enforcement. A new strategic approach and change management process are needed that operate within a workplace culture change framework. Workers need to feel that they can speak up and be heard safely and that they can actively participate in, and take responsibility for, change. The benefits of change must be effectively communicated and sold to all stakeholders through trusted leaders at the national, provincial and organisation level. The concept of change champions would be a potentially effective tool in Viet Nam where people are used to being unquestioningly guided by authority figures and where community leaders are proactively consulted and respected for their ability to provide instruction and advice on change, both personal and societal. As in any culture, however, change must be implemented at an appropriate pace but uncompromisingly to allow for a gradual but inevitable change of process, capacity and workplace culture. Viet Nam has a long cultural history, and to expect this to change overnight is unreasonable and a clear recipe for disaster.

In the News [14, 15]

The Government is addressing the rural health human resource drivers through policy and targeted incentive programs. "City doctors are offered up to US$2,300 to relocate but few are willing to move from the city where facilities and opportunities are greater. A new initiative will pilot a rotation model where provincial doctors will spend time in district and communal stations. This will be combined with local trainings to reduce the impact on treatment schedules and prevent further compounding the staff shortage problem."

Individual urban entities such as the Ho Chi Minh City Department of Health are mobilising their specialist medical practitioners and sending them to rural are as both to assist with improving capacity in district and communal stations and to ease the bottleneck in waiting lists. In December 2013, 37 doctors in the fields of intensive care, paediatrics, obstetrics and ENT were sent to assist 6 different hospitals. This has resulted in an extra 37,000 patients being treated and 130 doctors receiving training. This facilitates a greater capacity for local treatment which reduces the need to refer patients to other locations to receive their treatment.

References

1. Gordon S, Bernadett M, Evans D, Shapiro NB, Dang L (2009) Vietnamese culture: influences and implications for health care. Molina Health Care. Retrieved http://www.molinahealthcare.com/medicaid/providers/common/pdf/vietnameseculture-influences and implications for health care_material and test.pdf?E=true. Accessed 16 Sept 2014
2. Cam Quyen (2011) Patients "blackmailed" at hospitals http://english.vietnamnet.vn/fms/special-reports/12074/patients--blackmailed--at-hospitals.html. Accessed 16 Sept 2014
3. TUOI TRE NEWS (2014) Vietnam jails plastic surgeon for 19 years for dumping patient's body into river. Updated: 12/05/2014. http://tuoitrenews.vn/society/24492/killer-doctor-given-19-years-in-prison-for-dumping-body-into-river. Accessed 28 Sept 2014
4. DTINEWS (2014) Lack of license suspected in operation smile deaths. Posted on 28 Aug 2014 www.talkvietnam.com/2014/08/lack-of-license-suspected-in-operation-smile-deaths/. Accessed 28 Sept 2014
5. Nguyen M (2014) Vietnam preps for medical makeover to recoup lost billions in health care. Tue 14 Oct 2014. www.reuters.com/article/2014/10/14/vietnam-healthcare-idUSL3N0S33FD20141014. Accessed 9 Dec 2014
6. DTINEWS 2 (2014) Poor doctor care, lax security, blamed for hospital staff attacks. Posted on 8 Dec 2014. www.talkvietnam.com/2014/12/poor-doctor-care-lax-security-blamed-for-hospital-staff-attacks/. Accessed 9 Dec 2014
7. AmCham (2011) Tragedy at public hospitals. www.amchamvietnam.com/5364/tragedy-at-public-hospitals/. Accessed 28 Sept 2014
8. Ferriss AL (2010) Approaches to improving the quality of life: how to enhance the quality of life. Springer Science & Business Media, 2010. ISBN 9048191483, 9789048191482. 168 pages
9. Vietnam – Australian Oral Health Collaborative Initiatives (2010) Symposium on Vietnam-Australian Oral Health Initiatives 2010. www.oralhealthcrc.org.au/…/100514 VA symposium release.pdf. Accessed 10 Nov 2014
10. Nghiem Minh Association (2014) Mobile mental health support in Vietnam. Jan 2014. www.slideshare.net/loctran/mobile-mental-health-support-in-vietnam. Accessed 21 Aug 2014
11. Nguyen D, Hoang H, Hoang VM (2013) Public health in Vietnam: scientific evidence for policy changes and interventions. Editorial. Glob Health Action 2013 6: 20443. http://dx.doi.org/10.3402/gha.v610.20443. Accessed 05 Dec 2014

12. Vietnamese Family Health. Health beliefs and healing practices. www.vietfamilyhealth.org/culture/beliefs.html. Accessed 12 Jan 2015
13. Barroy H, Jarawan E, Balesd S (2014) Universal health coverage for inclusive and sustainable development. Country summary report for Vietnam. World Bank Group. Sept 2014. www.worldbank.org/en/topic/health/brief/uhc-japan. Accessed 10 Oct 2014
14. Viet Nam News (2014) Wednesday 2nd Jul 2014
15. Viet Nam News (2014) Saturday 5th Jul 2014

Chapter 4
The Infrastructure Landscape

Viet Nam currently (2014) has a population of 91.5 million with 70 % living in rural areas. Much of the population is not well serviced by infrastructure appropriate to support technology-driven health solutions or broadscale, integrated information systems of any kind. There is also no defined national health technology infrastructure or management strategy being implemented and no specialised training programmes in informatics or health technology. The Ministry of Health has however identified this as a focus for attention, but little measurable progress has been made to date outside of isolated pockets [1]. Viet Nam has a number of significant public health issues that could be addressed by e-health initiatives in particular as has occurred in so many other similar geographies. The key problem is how to develop and manage a sustainable, standardised, national health technology strategy and implementation framework. A number of significant barriers to progress have been identified including a lack of infrastructure, poor strategy development, a lack of co-ordinated effort towards defined goals, skills shortages in critical areas especially health information management, mobile technologies and security and a lack of cultural sensitivity by current research groups and funding bodies. Breaking down these barriers is critical to any future progress towards realising a viable health technology platform [2].

4.1 Capability

Viet Nam has approximately 1000 software outsourcing and IT businesses with most being small-sized businesses of 10–30 employees. There were 120,000 employees working in software and IT services in 2011 which was a 20-fold increase compared to 2002 [3]. 'In developed economies like the U.S. and European nations, IT accounts for some 7 % of gross domestic product (GDP), while the figure in Viet Nam is less than 2 %' [4]. Although behind the world figures for GDP, the annual growth rate was reportedly 25–35 % over the past 10 years for this industry segment

A.G. Shillabeer, *The Health of Vietnam*, DOI 10.1007/978-981-287-709-3_4

[3]. Due to this growth, the demand for IT specialists by outsourcers including IBM, Intel and Apple in particular has far exceeded the supply. Many outsourcing companies have been involved in global e-health technology development. These companies are gathering the best graduates and experienced staff available in Viet Nam and hence are developing the experience, knowledge and skills to provide healthcare solutions for Viet Nam.

To meet the need for skilled professionals, the number of universities and colleges offering a computing-focused program has grown over the past 10 years. There are currently 277 institutions with a total enrolment of 169,000 students, with 56,000 fresh students enrolling annually [3]. Whilst skills are becoming available, especially in the area of mobile technologies, there is currently no identified opportunity to specialise in health systems development or informatics. This is an obvious issue that needs to be addressed if Viet Nam is to progress in this area.

4.2 Technology Adoption

Research suggests that mobile phones are the most widely adopted form of technology in the world, including in developing countries [5, 6]. Data from Viet Nam showing that there are 143 mobile phones per 100 people clearly supports this claim [7]. Of those using mobile phones, 30 % use their phone to access the Internet, and 35 % use it for social networking [8]. Data for fixed-line Internet access shows that only 8/100 people across the world are connected, and in Viet Nam, the level is much lower at 4.3/100 [7]. There is a significant skew towards younger users with a reported 95 % of those aged 15–24 having Internet access of some form [8]. This is an important statistic as it has already been identified that most health information comes from older members of the community and family members, especially parents. The data on technology adoption suggests that these are the people least likely to have access to current, clinically accurate (if the correct sources are accessed) and appropriate information to counsel others with. Table 4.1 provides an overview of mobile technology adoption in Viet Nam.

The reliability of Vietnamese networks has been evaluated as 'suitable'. Testing shows that metrics such as successful call rate and service availability achieve over 99 % and complaints are measured at less than 0.1 % with 100 % response rate within 24 h [9].

There are a number of government initiatives that aim to strengthen the mobile/ Internet technology context in Viet Nam by 2015 including [10]:

- Licencing of 4G services
- Ensuring 40–45 % of households have a telephone and Internet access
- Providing mobile coverage to 90 % of the population

Since becoming officially connected to the global Internet network in 1997, the industry has grown significantly to currently support 19 Internet service providers,

Table 4.1 Mobile technology adoption [2, 4]

Metric	Value
Total domestic connection bandwidth	425,538 Mbps
Users per capita	35.58 %
Users	31,304,211
International connection bandwidth	346,997 Mbps
Domestic connection bandwidth	460,374 Mbps
Total VNIX network traffic	134,850,152 Gbytes
Dot VN active domain names	229,815
Allocated IPv4 addresses	15,551,232
Allocated IPv6 addresses	73,015,820,288/64
Total broadband subscribers	4,325,995
3G phone subscribers/100 people	8.5
3G service coverage	30 cities and provinces
Number of 2G/3G cell sites in the south-west	7100

1064 licenced websites and 335 social networking sites. 3G Internet users account for 18 % of the population [9].

Viet Nam is ready for the application of health technologies and mobile technologies in particular given that it has reasonably good literacy rates as shown in Table 4.1, the number of technology graduates in the workplace is growing, there is a high level of technology uptake and reliability of infrastructure is good. Most importantly, Viet Nam is experiencing a strong drive towards technology adoption, local development and desire for social equity with other countries in the health domain [2].

4.3 Health Information Systems Integration

Viet Nam has a group specifically created to work on building development and research capacity in health technology. The main objectives of the Health Technology Adoption (HTA) group are to [11]:

- Build and develop HTA-related capacities of academia, researchers, health technology producers, supplier, purchasers, patients and other stakeholders of health system in Viet Nam
- Support the development and exchange of HTA-related information, methods, expertise and ideas
- Enhance the use of HTA-related scientific evidence in decision-making in health systems in Viet Nam
- Network with other relevant institutions/organisations in Viet Nam and in other countries to promote HTA agenda in Viet Nam as well as in the world

The HTA has also defined a quality information system as one 'that guarantees supply, analysis and dissemination of reliable health information to policy makers at all levels of the health system regularly and on an ad hoc basis' [11].

One would expect that having such a focused group that health information systems would be reasonably good; however, this is not yet the case. At present, health statistics are collected from the routine reporting systems at each location and from surveys. Routine health data collection is conducted at all levels of the health system, from the MOH to the commune level, using standardised forms. Unfortunately, this work remains largely paper based and creates a considerable workload for health workers, especially at the communal level. Furthermore, national health target programmes have their own reporting forms and registers from the communal level up. Every year, the MOH publishes an Annual Health Statistics Yearbook that reflects health outcomes and performance. Information is collected and collated from routine, hard copy reports of 63 provinces/cities, national health target programmes, departments and institutions.

In the hospital system, the MOH has developed a software called *Medisoft* and disseminated this software to all public hospitals. However, the application of this software faces major challenges, partly because hospitals do not have sufficient infrastructure, e.g. computer and appropriate personnel, and partly because this software is unable to meet the current requirements for hospital management, especially in the context of autonomisation. Currently, many hospitals use different hospital management software.

With regard to outbreak detection and monitoring, Viet Nam has a preventive medicine system that operates very well on collection, surveying, disseminating and using statistical data on epidemiology to assist in effective control of dangerous epidemics like SARS, avian influenza A/H5N1 and most recently pandemic influenza A/H1N1, as well as for monitoring the national health target programmes [11].

With regard to data synthesis, the number of experts in the health sector and related agencies that have received training on quantitative analysis skills has increased considerably in the past few years. However, to be able to truly leverage the power of informatics, these 'experts' need to accumulate many years of experience to acquire the skills to use data effectively to analyse and assess health problems and policies [6, 11]. There is also a call to standardise data collection and formats; however, this work is still being scoped with input from the Asian Development Bank and other similar organisations.

4.3.1 Technology Policy Changes

Health information system management in the recent past has suffered from many limitations including a lack of focused activities and inadequate implementation. On February 25, 2009, the Ministry of Health issued a Directive 02/CT-BYT on promoting application and development of health information technology in every area of work: from governance, storage and information exchange to administrative reform [6]. The Directive indicated that depending on local conditions, each facility should allocate at least 1 % of its revenue to pay for the application and development of information technology including the databases of each health facility. Central and provincial hospitals were requested to apply hospital management software before 2010. Whilst governance and information exchange between the Ministry, units under its direct supervision and provincial health bureaus has been strengthened and implemented, unfortunately, there has been little other measured or reported progress [6, 8, 12]. The Science and Training Department of the MOH has several projects to provide evidence to policymakers regarding the benefits of information systems implementation, and there is increased attention on using information in policymaking, but this is one of several areas of priority that is constantly listed but never achieved.

4.3.2 Major Difficulties and Challenges

Of the six building blocks of the Vietnamese health system, the health information system is the weakest component [12]. The health information system is evaluated according to the following contents: governance and policy development, resources, data collection and quality of information, data analysis and use of information [13]:

- *Governance and policy*: The MOH has enacted regulations on health information for all levels. However, co-ordination, integration of the different units and intermediaries of the health information system remain unclear. Penalties and incentives are inadequate. There is no regulation that mandates public and private health facilities to report data to serve the national health information system.
- *Resources*: Investment in health information systems is poor and irregular with insufficient supporting equipment. There is a shortage of information technology staff, whilst those who are working have poor technical skills, especially at the grass-roots level.
- *Data collection and quality*: There is a lack of co-ordination, sharing of information within and between sectors and across health programmes and an overlap of information collected and analysed. Information on the same indicators varies between different ministries and sectors; often, it is not available and cannot be used for planning purposes. There is no guidance and criteria for data collection and reporting. Many databases are collected from small samples that are not sufficiently representative. There is a shortage of data disaggregation by sex, age, ethnicity and disadvantaged regions to allow assessment of policy impacts.
- *Data analysis*: Very weak at all levels, especially the grass-roots level, due to shortage of personnel with specialised skills in data processing and analysis. Data analysis is done without unified and integrated methods. In addition, results differ for the same health indicator across different sources of data, which further complicates data analysis work.
- *Use of health information*: Limited because of the absence of guidance and regulations on the use of information for health planning purposes at all levels.

Dissemination of materials is predominantly for internal use only with almost no external access to the data or reports in many cases. This prevents transparency and independent evaluation or critique. Awareness of the importance of the utilisation of information to improve healthcare and develop an evidence-based foundation for health planning and strategy is still low at the management level. Most health managers have not had any training in data management or informatics [13].

4.4 Medisoft

Medisoft was developed specifically for implementation in Viet Nam through the various health departments and is currently the only system promoted for general use by the Ministry of Health. Its development was initiated by Dr Vu Manh Tien, previously a clinician at the Children's Hospital. In 1995, the project received $60,000 seed funding from Marina Picasso (grandchild of the artist Picasso) to support the development of technical and networking infrastructure. The first release was made available in 1997. The program was designed to facilitate management of the whole patient lifecycle from admission to hospital through recording procedures and costs, medication dispensing and other services until discharge. It was also designed to be the 'single source of truth' for a patient, and therefore, all history would be available to the treating clinician upon re-examination or admission events.

On May 12, 2007, around the time of the release of the latest version, Dr Tien allowed the source code for Medisoft 2003 to be made available and free on the Internet. He wanted to make the software available to countries whose economies constrain or prevent the implementation of expensive international software solutions [14]. The clinical training and reference functions and documents remain fully open source and downloadable as is a demo version of both the 2003 and 2007 versions of the software [15].

The system implemented Viet Nam-specific functionality including the ability to manage Vietnamese specific guidelines, e.g. free treatment if under age 6, medical insurance management and training functions including images for diagnostic training, vaccine administration guidelines, knowledge testing, pandemic readiness procedures and most importantly integration of IDC10 codes in English and Vietnamese [14].

The full cost of this software including accounting, networking, claims processing and reporting functions and system training materials is $8345 not including monthly service contracts and database licences which are between $299 and $8269 depending upon the number of users [16].

The software has not been implemented nationally, and there is still a great deal of fragmentation, inconsistency and incompatibility between health software installations across the country as shown in Table 4.2. This presents obvious problems in terms of data management and utilisation.

Table 4.2 HIT infrastructure

Healthcare level	HIT infrastructure
National/central hospitals	Many top-level hospitals in Viet Nam have individual health information systems. The quality and daily usage of these systems vary. Most of these systems incorporate in some way Medisoft 2003 software developed by the Ministry of Health for hospitals at all levels to send statistics and reports to the Ministry's Department of Therapy
Provincial hospitals	Provincial hospitals generally have IT networks, as well as some health information systems with linked databases for patient master indices, consultations and emergency, finance and pharmacy
District hospitals and commune health centres	District and commune health centres tend to have just a few computers with dial-up Internet connections. Lower-level units derive much of their general medical information from television and newspaper and via training courses. Together with the United Nations Development Programme, the Ministry of Health's Department of Financial Planning developed software for district and commune health information system management; however, this software is not yet widely used

4.5 Technology Challenges

There are a number of significant challenges facing Viet Nam if it wishes to implement broadscale technology solutions to health. These challenges can be grouped into five categories as presented in the following table (Table 4.3).

In the News [17]

The health system in the central provinces of Nghe An lacks both equipment and manpower according to health experts

"The mountainous Truong Duong District has 18 commune medical stations but most of them have been downgraded and lack necessary equipment" said Pham Quoc Duong, Director of the Truong Duong Medical Station. "So there are many difficulties in carrying out medical examinations and treating people."

About 67,000 residents have registered for health checks at medical stations in communes and towns. "There are too many people for the amount of infrastructure", Duong said.

"For instance, at Xa Luong Commune Medical Station, which is five kilometres from the district centre, buildings are run down, electricity often does not work and there is little or no water. If medical workers need clean water to wash their hands they much take it from a stream" said Duong.

Hun Vi Truong, a doctor at the Quy Chau District Medical Station said that "medical equipment was issued a long time ago and it rarely worked. Some of it was forgotten and covered with dust."

Table 4.3 HIT challenges

Challenge	Description
Unified policy direction	There are both conflicting and overlapping policies and gaps in policies to guide the procurement, implementation and management of technology in healthcare leading to difficulties in compliance and an inability to sustain and monitor infrastructure
Skilled HIT technicians	Whilst there is great interest among health workers in Viet Nam at all levels of the health system, the majority of the population is unaware of the vast potential of HIT. There are also very few training opportunities and even fewer with the skills and knowledge required to develop and deliver training
Infrastructure and resources	There is a shortage of stable IT network connections throughout Viet Nam, especially in rural areas and in small health centres. Although mobile phones are prevalent in cities, they are not as widespread in rural areas; as a result, the use of telemedicine and mobile phones as key infrastructure for HIT may not be feasible. Also, when simply ensuring there are sufficient medical practitioners to treat patients and providing accurate diagnoses and referrals in time to save lives is an almost insurmountable problem, investing in high-tech solutions becomes a very low priority
Cost	For a health centre, the cost of one computer alone can be prohibitively high, not to mention the cost of a network of computers and technicians to keep them running. Most hospitals and health centres have very limited budgets for HIT operation and maintenance. Software is also expensive, especially the cost of the software's copyright
Standards	HIT software is not standardised at each point of care; as a result, some hospitals must enter a patient's information repeatedly in different programs, thus introducing errors. There are no national data minimum sets for Viet Nam, little or no compatibility between systems and no real understanding of the application of data to healthcare

References

1. Pham HMT, Vo HKT (2006) HIT case study. Center for Health and Aging. Health Information Technology and Policy Lab, Vietnam
2. Shillabeer A (2013) Development of an E-health strategic framework for Vietnam. Chapter 19, pp 163–173. In: Mandal P (ed) Proceedings of the international conference on managing the Asian century: ICMAC 2013. Springer Science & Business Media, 2014. ISBN 9814560618, 9789814560610. 668 Pages
3. Nghiem Minh Association (2014) Mobile mental health support in Vietnam. Jan 2014. www.slideshare.net/loctran/mobile-mental-health-support-in-vietnam. Accessed 21 Aug 2014
4. Nguyen NTT, Tran LK, Bui LN, Theo V, Nguyen HT, Ngo AD (2008) Estimation of Vietnam national burden of disease 2008. Asia Pac J Public Health. doi:10.1177/1010539513510556
5. Tran H, Pretorius R (2008). Vietnameses [sic] medical education and development of family medicine in Vietnam. State University of New York at Buffalo School of Medicine and Biomedical Sciences. VMGUS Publication No 052009, New York
6. United Nations (2011) Viet Nam annual report 2011. May 2011. www.un.org.vn. Accessed 10 Oct 2014
7. Nguyen D, Hoang H, Hoang VM (2013) Public health in Vietnam: scientific evidence for policy changes and interventions. Editorial. Glob Health Action 2013 6:20443. http://dx.doi.org/10.3402/gha.v610.20443. Accessed 12 May 2014

8. U.S. Government Global Health Initiative Strategy (2011). U.S. Government in Washington, Vietnam V5.0. Aug 2011
9. Barroy H, Jarawan E, Balesd S (2014) Universal health coverage for inclusive and sustainable development. Country summary report for Vietnam. World Bank Group. Sept, 2014. www.worldbank.org/en/topic/health/brief/uhc-japan. Accessed 10 Oct 2014
10. Marriott A (2011) Vietnam's health care system suffers on policy failure. Global Health Check. www.globalhealthcheck.org/?p=423. Accessed 19 Aug 2014
11. Hoang MV (2013) Introducing health technology assessment interest group in Vietnam (HTA-VN). Center for Health System Research, Hanoi Medical University, Hanoi
12. Nguyen VT, Ha DA, Tran MO, Prakongsai P, Tangcharoensathien V (2011) The independent assessment of the process and the content of the five year health plan, 2011–15. In: Vietnam. Final report 7 Jan 2011. Ministry of Health of Viet Nam, Health Partnerships Group, Joint Annual Health Review 2011, Hanoi
13. Nghiem DT (2010) Social health insurance in Viet Nam. Health Insurance Department, Ministry of Health, Ha Noi, 12 Oct 2010. http://www.ilo.org/wcmsp5/groups/public/---asia/---ro-bangkok/---ilo-hanoi/documents/presentation/wcms_145792.pdf. Accessed 10 Nov 2014
14. The Business Forum Newspaper (2012) The paving the way for health informatics platform. Chief Editor: Pham Ngoc Tuan. Thursday, 4 Oct 2012
15. Medisoft (2007) http://www.medisoft.com.vn/moresoft2.htm. Accessed 2 Oct 2014
16. SLC Software. www.slcsoftware.com/prices.asp. Accessed 2 Oct 2014
17. Viet Nam News (2014) Wednesday 2 July 2014

[illegible] Government [illegible] Health [illegible] [illegible] in Washington [illegible] Vietnam [illegible] Aug 2011 [illegible]
9. [illegible] (2011) [illegible] [illegible] [illegible] [illegible] [illegible] [illegible] [illegible] [illegible] [illegible] 2011 [illegible]
10. [illegible] (2011) [illegible] [illegible] [illegible] globalhealth [illegible] Accessed [illegible] Aug 2016
11. [illegible] MV [illegible] [illegible] [illegible] [illegible] [illegible] HHS [illegible] [illegible] [illegible] [illegible] [illegible]
12. [illegible] VT, Ha [illegible], Tran [illegible] (2011) [illegible] [illegible] [illegible] [illegible] content of the [illegible] [illegible] [illegible] 2012. Ministry of Health of Viet Nam. Health [illegible] Annual Health Review 2011 [illegible]
13. Nguyen [illegible] (2010) Social health insurance in Viet Nam [illegible] Ministry of Health [illegible] Vol. 17 [illegible] 2010 [illegible] [illegible] Accessed 10 [illegible]
14. Business Forum Newspaper (2012) The [illegible] [illegible] [illegible] [illegible]
15. [illegible] (2011) [illegible] [illegible] [illegible] [illegible] 2011 [illegible]

Chapter 5
Current Status

5.1 Stakeholders Influencing Vietnamese Healthcare

There are four groups of influential stakeholders in Vietnamese health policy and strategy. At the top are the various authorising ministries with the Ministry of Health having governance over strategy development and the Ministry of Planning and Finance having authority over allocating budget. Final approval and authority to proceed with any initiative and policy release comes from the Prime Minister. Below the ministerial level are the key advisory groups that provide inputs in the form of policy and health strategy expertise, development methodology evaluations and process audits. Then there is a level of stakeholder that does not influence the inputs or processing/implementation of health directives or strategy but has significant influence over the outputs of a plan or strategy. This is achieved through defining the broad research foci and identifying targeted programmes of work aimed at achieving the goals set by the higher levels of influence.

One of the most influential players in the Vietnamese healthcare policy domain (outside of the ministries) is the Health Partnership Group (HPG). The primary function of this group is to provide an independent evaluation and assessment of the development methodology and implementation of each 5-year national health plan [1].

Participation in the Health Partnership Group is by invitation only and includes universities, NGOs and major health organisations both commercial and non-commercial. Interested parties need to send a letter of recommendation from their organisation and there may be an MOU required as part of the request. There are a number of universities providing research and medical expertise to the HPG including Hanoi Medical University, HCMC Medical and Pharmacy University and the National Institute of Hygiene and Epidemiology but as of the end of 2014 there were no international universities represented. The Director of the International Cooperation Department (ICD) considers all applications and communicates the result of the discussion back to the applicant. If successful a formal invitation is provided. An application to register as a participant is usually decided upon very

A.G. Shillabeer, *The Health of Vietnam*, DOI 10.1007/978-981-287-709-3_5

quickly and this process can be completed in as little as a week. Any significant local or international organisation with an interest in health is eligible to register [2]. This facilitates a broad range of input and a highly democratic process to be applied to this important process that directly impacts upon the healthcare policy and provision of services over the 5 years in which the plan applies. Whilst the HPG does not directly influence policy, it does have significant input to evaluating the results and achievements and the methodology for developing, implementing and assessing the plans which provides transparency and trust in the process and plan as a whole.

HPG meetings are scheduled by the ICD which sits within the Ministry of Health. There are usually four meetings a year and they are co-chaired by the Minister of Health or Vice Minister and one high-level representative such as an ambassador or department head from a development partner.

Whilst the HPG has an overarching function as described above, it also has subgroups that focus on particular areas of the healthcare platform and plan, for example, information technology [2]. IT is also one of the priorities of the Ministry of Health and this is to be addressed through an IT strengthening strategy for the health sector. There are currently (2015) two technical working groups (TWG) within the HPG focusing on IT [3]. One is focusing on HMIS development and implementation and one general IT focus group with the aim of supporting the ministry to address their strategy of integrating a range of information systems and technology solutions into the Vietnamese health landscape. There are a number of other working groups to address the other priority areas for the ministry and provide an opportunity for a range of expertise to be involved.

The second key group in monitoring and assessing the 5-year health plan is the Joint Assessment of the National Strategies (JANS) team. The team is composed of four Vietnamese nationals and two international experts and provides recommendations to the ministry regarding the development and content of each national plan and the plans at the provincial level which represent the implementation of the national strategy. The JANS team assesses each draft of the plan against a set of 21 attributes [1]. The assessment output is a comprehensive report detailing feedback and recommendations to be incorporated into the next draft. The team also performs a final assessment on the plan that is signed into operation by the Prime Minister.

In contrast to the HPG, which acts as a think tank for strategy development, the JANS team is not involved in any aspect of developing the plan. This enables the team to fulfil its function without potential for suggestion of conflict of interest and therefore is able to transparently provide an independent assessment of the process and content of the plan.

There are a number of unaffiliated independent groups with broad representation that manage strategic projects and provide expert input, often through the HPG, to the strategy and policy development process. One such organisation is the internationally managed NGO centre based in Hanoi. Similar to the HPG, this group is composed of members all of which are international non-governmental organisations.

To apply for membership, organisations must be licenced to operate in Viet Nam and present a copy of the business registration certificate issued by the People's Aid

Coordinating Committee (PACCOM). Individuals and other partners are allowed to join discussions and meetings of the centre and working groups but cannot become members [4].

The NGO centre not only focuses on health but also has working groups focusing on 40 programmatic sectors including climate change, microfinance, ethnic minorities, disaster management, child rights, Agent Orange, etc. The centre is essentially a facilitator for high-level meetings and discussions that aim to influence policy and programmes but the centre does not independently get directly involved in strategy or programme development or implementation.

Input to health policy, strategy and implementation is also sought from global players such as the WHO and UN and international universities. These groups can be very influential but usually provide short-term focused input through working groups or fixed-contract expertise supply. This form of engagement is not easy to secure and requires strong relationships and trust to be established.

The Viet Nam Public Health Association (VPHA) is the only active group founded by Vietnamese that targets population health issues and hosts networking and professional development events [5]. Their primary focus is on providing an advocacy and education function in through the Viet Nam Journal of Public Health which they publish in English. As such they indirectly influence health projects and strategy but they are important as they are unique in providing exposure for Vietnamese research outputs in the English-speaking world.

The VPHA are also one of the few Vietnamese groups that develop and implement national and provincial projects with local management and funding. Their projects are commonly developed in response to national strategies as documented by the ministry. Projects have previously included the 'elderly health promotion program in Tien Hai' and a 'smoke-free cities in Nha Trang and Hue' initiative in line with the national tobacco control policy [5]. The elderly health project was judged one of the top five innovations to assist with improving the health and activity levels of the elderly by the International Federation on Ageing in 2013. They are also active collaborators on projects such as One Health which focuses on interdisciplinary approaches to sustainable human, animal and ecosystem health and dioxin exposure management with the Queensland University of Technology.

Whilst the groups discussed above have their roots locally, there are also a number of international players with policy and strategic influence especially from the US and Australia. These players seek to develop projects that directly address ministerial strategies and work within the framework documented in the Viet Nam Global Health Strategy [6] in particular. The GHS was created in response to the identified areas of focus for health improvement in Viet Nam and was a collaborative publication by Chemonics International, the United Nations, ABT Associates, Harvard Medical School AIDS Initiative in Vietnam and Management Sciences for Health. Together with the Millennium Development Goals, the GHS is a broad reference point for researchers looking to make an impact on public health in Viet Nam. Whilst these documents and collaborations do not influence the strategic direction of healthcare in Viet Nam, the information they provide has the potential to significantly influence research directions and improvements in the provision of healthcare and health outcomes. Importantly they identify areas of significance for the government and hence the areas that are most likely to receive ministry support and be sustainable.

Any new or external groups looking to provide recognised benefit or develop credibility in Viet Nam would be advised to consider investing in any opportunities to engage with the groups discussed here or to focus on targeted areas for focus and investment by the Vietnamese Government.

5.2 Financial Platform and Reforms

Viet Nam underwent almost complete political and economic reform in the late 1980s through a process known as Doi Moi. This has resulted in economic growth of almost 8 % per annum and economic sustainability for Viet Nam [7]. Whilst there have also been sustained improvements in healthcare outcomes nationally, there have also been underlying effects to the healthcare system that have not been so positive. Doi Moi triggered greater local and overseas health investment particularly in areas concerning pharmacology, with one local manufacturing entity being established and private clinics and hospitals being built with expert human resources being employed to raise capacity and broaden service provision. Even with this local capacity building and expanded range of medical service provision, universal health coverage was still reportedly only at 64 % in 2012 and this is a focus for future political and economic reform [7]. The benefit has not been felt by a significant proportion of the population. Not surprisingly the least benefit has been felt by those most in need, the elderly and those in rural and poor communities [8, 9]. The natural feelings of disenfranchisement are further exacerbated by evidence suggesting that there has also been a measured shift in fiscal burden for healthcare services from the state to the individual therefore creating a barrier to access where options and availability have been opened up. The net result is reportedly lowered access and higher cost for those that stood to potentially gain the most from the 30 years of financial reforms [8].

The most obvious effect of fiscal policy reform since Doi Moi is the huge growth in the private health sector [6]. Whilst there are a small number of larger private hospitals being built such as the locally funded Vinmec in Hanoi, most facilities are relatively small, specialised and located primarily in major cities and affluent areas where potential patients could afford the fees charged. Private facilities are often staffed by the same professionals who work in public facilities suggesting the same skills and experience are applied but the level of technology and infrastructure is usually newer and compliant with global gold standards. Growth in the private sector is expected to steadily increase in line with growth in GDP and average incomes [6].

Less obvious at the street level but equally important as a landscape change trigger is the implementation of global standards to drug manufacturing in Viet Nam. This provides employment opportunities and a reduction in financial barriers to supply both local and potentially regional markets for some medications. Given its large population Viet Nam has a sustainable market to support a medication supply industry into the future. Estimates suggest that the compound annual growth rate in medication spending is around 16 % in local terms and grew from 3.3 bn USD in 2013 to 3.92 bn USD in 2014. In comparison, healthcare spending grew by 14.7 % in local terms from 10.94 bn USD to 12.8 bn USD over the same period [10]. This growth is expected to continue into the medium term and presents an attractive opportunity for both local entrepreneurs and international investors. The Vietnamese Government is looking to supply 80 % of the local market by 2020 and has already invested 10 m USD into building a new manufacturing plant in Bac Ninh which is compliant with WHO standards [10]. The following is a high-level overview of the key changes in health financing in Viet Nam over the past 30 years [11]:

- Until end of 1980s: health care funded and provided by the government, but very limited resources
- 1989: User fees introduced at public health facilities
- 1992: Introduction of social health insurance
- 2002: set up Health Care Fund for the poor
- 2005: Free care for children under 6 years
- 2008: Law on SHI passed, in effect on 1 July 2009

5.2.1 Access Versus Utilisation

There is currently disparity between the cost of service provision between the public and private sector that divides the population demographics and creates a skewed perception of the quality of service. The services are often very comparable between the two structures; however, private services cost well beyond those of the public sector and are utilised by wealthier patients. In other industries such as fashion, electronics and cars, this increased cost and demographic attraction suggests better product quality, but this is not necessarily the case in healthcare (especially when as noted earlier the same treating professionals are often practicing across both sectors) and serves to obfuscate the true measure of quality of local healthcare provision. Whilst those accessing the more expensive, private facilities may believe they are getting better treatment, the data suggests that increased access to, and quality of, healthcare services has resulted in improved outcomes across the whole of Viet Nam in the past 30 years. The precise numbers are hard to determine however due to unreliable and inconsistent data collection across the country [8]. Work by the World Bank suggests that the key areas of improvement over the past 10 years have been in child and maternal health including a decline in infant mortality from 30 to 16 per 100,000 live births and under-five mortality rates reducing from 42 to 25 per 100,000 [7].

At an individual level there is a double-edged effect of the distorted perception of quality: the first is that it is believed that high-quality healthcare is out of reach for most; the second is that informal payments are required to receive timely and good treatment and hence the actual cost exceeds the advertised cost. The first of these beliefs is somewhat driven by financial reports showing that out-of-pocket expenses had risen to 80 % in the first 10 years of Doi Moi and are still between 59 % and 70 % [8]. Even for the 60 % of the population with private insurance, there is the suggestion of significant expense that must be borne by the individual and the amount to be found is not always clear and hence presents a significant financial risk for those in lower socio-demographic groups. Many risk falling into poverty even by seeking treatment for relatively minor health incidents. Interestingly, treatments for areas of focus for the government such as TB are either free or very low cost but this information is not widely known and many suffer needlessly and potentially spread preventable disease by not accessing treatments early or at all [12]. This treatment avoidance behaviour increases the burden on financial management and service provision across the health industry.

The issue of informal or 'envelope' payments is also not without evidence to substantiate the belief. Although not condoned by government bodies that manage the health providers, a recent survey showed that 65 % of health service users encountered unethical financial requests or expectations by medical professionals and 70 % of professionals admitted to asking patients for 'bribes' to facilitate better or faster attention [12]. Whilst these payments would be considered very small to most of us from western countries, they represent a measurable proportion of the weekly or monthly income for those in disadvantaged areas and hence present a real barrier to health-seeking activities. There are also 'invisible' informal payments through the practice of overprescribing medications which already have prices inflated by up to 30 % [8]. Given that the proportion of personal health costs attributable to medication is 45–60 % of all costs, the effect of invisible inflation is significant and only serves to further increase the barrier to healthcare access for the average Vietnamese. Even when physical access is universal, the ability to take advantage of that availability becomes less and less feasible when the confounding issues are factored in. Considering all of the extra costs mentioned above, it is no surprise that participation in the health system is still very low in regional and mountainous areas and for those from lower socio-demographic groups, which is, in fact, most of the non-urban population. This means that income to the health system is also lowered overall and the potential to invest in national health programmes and evidence improvements in rural outcomes (where rates of people seeking treatment and hence being 'cured' are lower) is also minimised, creating somewhat of a vicious circle and a growing negative health mythology.

Another significant, direct impact of the access or, more correctly, utilisation disparity is the placement of investment which is commonly skewed towards the private/urban sector as it presents a much stronger business case and ROI potential. On paper at least, it is a significantly better investment where there is a patient population that could afford to pay for expensive technology-driven health solutions and hence provide a financial return in a reasonable time. In 2011 public spending on health was measured at 6.4 % of GDP but 70 % of funding was targeted at the provincial level [10]. Most spending was aimed towards curative rather than preventative or educational initiatives which could provide a more long-term, rather than diagnosis-based, benefit and provide a positive impact on health finance and national outcomes into the mid and long term. Disparity in utilisation of health services has been measured by the World Bank and in September 2014 the following breakdown was reported [7]:

Outpatient visits:

- Forty percent at private or traditional facilities
- Thirty-seven percent at state run hospitals
- Twenty-three percent at commune or provincial-level health clinics

Inpatient care:

- 5.4 % in private facilities
- Eighty-three percent in state run hospitals
- Eleven percent in commune or provincial-level health clinics

Overall health spending in Viet Nam has grown at an average rate of 9.8 % since 1998 which is 2.6 % above growth in GDP [13]. The following represents the breakdown in health spending [13]:

Household out of pocket	55.5 %
Social health insurance	14.2 %
Central government budget	3.7 %
Provincial government budget	19 %
Other private spending	6.3 %
Other	1.3 %

5.2.2 *Social Health Insurance*

In response to the Vietnamese Constitution of 1992, which declared that it is a legal right of all citizens to receive health protection and access to healthcare, a national social health insurance (SHI) programme was launched in 1993 [7]. Realising that this programme was out of reach for minorities and poor population segments, an auxiliary healthcare fund for the poor (HCFP) was created which provided a basic level of cover and access to free or low-cost healthcare services for the whole population without financial contribution. These two initiatives were rolled together in 2005 and a new health insurance law was passed in November 2008 and effected on July 1, 2009 [7, 11]. There is also a voluntary insurance programme for dependants of those in the compulsory programme; however, this programme is suffering from self-selection as those taking advantage are most frequently those with current health issues that would most benefit from the insurance coverage provided [11]. The voluntary programme is therefore a low return venture for the government and presents a significant financial burden on the managing ministries.

There are currently 63 provincial funds to cover Viet Nam and 25 categories of compulsory coverage as listed below. The coverage categories represent defined groups of people that are required to have SHI coverage with a defined copayment from between 0 % and 20 % depending upon the category the individual is covered by [13].

1. Workers, managers of enterprises, and civil servants
2. Officers of the Ministry of Public Security
3. Pensioners
4. Persons who are beneficiaries of a monthly social security allowance due to occupational injuries and diseases
5. Workers who stopped receiving the disability allowance or were rubber workers and who now receive a monthly allowance from the government budget
6. Retired commune civil servants who receive a monthly social security allowance
7. Retired commune staff who receive a monthly social security allowance from the government
8. Unemployed persons who receive an unemployment allowance according to the law on unemployment
9. Persons awarded for revolutionary merit
10. Veterans who served before April 30, 1975, and youth volunteers during the war against the French
11. People who directly served in the war against the USA
12. Members of the National Assembly and People's Committees
13. Persons who receive a monthly social protection allowance
14. The very poor and members of ethnic minorities living in disadvantaged areas
15. Dependants of persons awarded for revolutionary merit
16. Dependants of officers from the Ministry of Defence and the Ministry of Public Security
17. Children under 6 years of age
18. Organ donors
19. Foreigners studying in Viet Nam on Vietnamese Government fellowships
20. Poor households
21. School children and students
22. Agriculture households
23. Dependants of formal-sector workers
24. Members of cooperatives and family enterprises
25. Workers on sick leave who need long-term treatment for specific diseases as defined by the health minister

Whilst SHI coverage is broad and aims to cover all those who can either afford the premiums and hence should contribute to the cost of health services (through premiums and copayments) or who are deserving of government support such as the poor and children, only 17 % of the possible 64 % of the population were covered by 2010 [7]. The net result of this is a lack of funding for proposed programmes, especially in the management of non-communicable diseases. Whilst state funding is legally bound to subsidise insurance for large population groups, funding for minorities and smaller population groups remains discretionary [7] and in times of finding constraints it is those in most need that are likely to be hardest hit as a result. Unfortunately this complex scenario calls for a sustained heavy reliance on out-of-pocket payments for all users to cover even basic costs. Whilst out-of-pocket expenses have reportedly dropped from a high of 63 %, there is still a catastrophic financial impact for 7.8 % of those in the lowest socio-demographic quartile and impoverishment resulting for 7.5 % of the same group compared to 5.5 % across all groups [7]. These out-of-pocket expenses are predominantly incurred for treatment at public or private facilities (66 %) and self-medication expenses (35 %) with treatment costs going up by more than double and medication costs reducing by around half in the 5 years to 2010 [7].

Total health expenditure represents 6.4 % of GDP or around 45 USD per capita and is attributed as follows [11]:

- 12 USD public funded: 26.2 %
- 28 USD per household: 62.8 %
- 5 USD from other sources: 11 %

The Ministry of Health defined a road map to guide Viet Nam (Fig. 5.1) in universal health insurance coverage; however, given the current scenario it will not be achieved until some time later than predicted although the component constructs are in place [11].

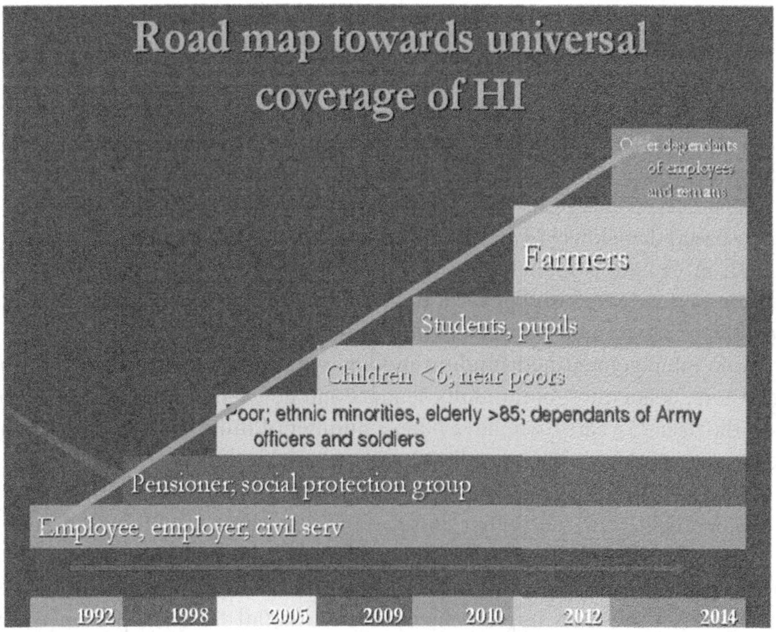

Fig. 5.1 Vietnamese Government road map for improving health insurance coverage [11]

5.3 Healthcare Policy and Programmes

Doi Moi and the subsequent financial investment in healthcare in Viet Nam saw outcomes and coverage improve and triggered a new focus on public health and prevention for the first time [14]. This change of focus and in a direction where there is little applied expertise in Viet Nam has slowed the pace of progress and whilst there have been achievements especially in child and maternal health many long-term health problems are still prevalent including HIV, malaria and dengue fever [14, 15]. New problems such as non-communicable diseases and in particular the increasing incidence of cardiovascular disease, conditions related to aging, alcoholism and diabetes to mention but a few have placed an increasing burden on the healthcare system and policymakers who are often dealing with many unknowns simultaneously. Whilst every effort is being made to ensure quality service, access for all and monitoring and controls provided, it is an almost intractable problem when the environment is constantly and rapidly changing and increased funding requirements and local skills and knowledge cannot keep pace.

It is believed that whilst policy and ministerial decrees can assist in improving healthcare infrastructure, quality, affordability and access, there is a strong call for basic education to raise the levels of health literacy among the less advantaged Vietnamese population segments. Reports suggest that in areas of public health such as alcohol use and smoking, there is a large financial cost but little general knowledge about the harmful effects of participating in these activities [16]. Taxes on tobacco products are also relatively low and present little barrier to participation and little revenue to treat the consequences [7]. Therefore, a multilevel approach, with international expertise where required, is needed for sustained and measurable improvements to be realised. There is also a need for all stakeholders to come to the table and agree on a broad collaborative approach to be implemented across all levels of the healthcare system from individual education programmes to national regulatory and other controls. Whilst stakeholders are aware of the need for change, there is a perceived lack of information or information capacity upon which to make evidence-based decisions [14]. The capacity, access and skills in using and developing health information systems are therefore integral to the change process as is integration of academics and general data scientists. Unfortunately it is often difficult to achieve agreement between different ministerial groups on implementation, programme management and funding models without bringing healthcare providers, investors, academics, community leaders and new technologies into the fray.

Over the past 25 years there have been a number of ministerial decrees on health. These decrees underpin the overall strategic plans by the federal government and are implemented through successive 5-year plans. Between plans there are many decrees, directives, laws and other enforceable guidelines developed in health and each 5-year plan incorporates all of these and they are essentially put into effect when the plan is released. The 5-year plans outline the broad national health strategies which are then implemented in more detail by each province. During development, each plan is evaluated and revised many times by different stakeholders and independent groups prior to release to ensure legitimacy and applicability. This is an important quality mechanism in ensuring plans are implementable and measurable and provide benefit across the country but they do not ensure that all strategies will actually be implemented. After development and release a process of annual reviews, compliance and implementation is assessed and reported, and areas for future legal, social or clinical attention are identified.

5.3.1 The 5-Year Health Plan

The most recent active health plan was released into operation on December 25, 2010 [1]. This plan was written to guide the strategic direction for healthcare policy and implementation from 2010 to 2015 and is written around five health pillars: health workforce; the health financing system; the health information system; medical products, vaccines and technologies and leadership and governance. Each of these pillars has a defined focus [1, 6]:

- The health workforce will be competent, responsive, fair and efficient in order to achieve the best health outcomes across all regions. There will be a focus on sustainability and development of human resources for health (HRH) in rural, remote and low-accessibility areas. Quantity and quality of village health workers, community health workers and district health centre staff will receive particular attention.
- The health financing system will provide adequate funds to ensure all people can access and use healthcare services and are protected from financial catastrophe or impoverishment associated with health costs. The health financing system will increase public spending for health, reduce out-of-pocket costs and manage the health budget more effectively.
- The health information system should provide reliable and timely information on health status, health determinates and health system performance for use by provincial or national health managers. The information, education and communication (IEC) programmes will be strengthened to facilitate and enhance all health activities.
- Medical products, vaccines and technologies are critical components of the health system and must be of high quality, safe, scientifically sound and cost effective.
- Leadership and governance includes regulation, oversight, coalition building, attention to system design, accountability, education and training for health system managers at all levels, in order to implement, monitor and enforce health sector reform consistent with the national policy.

The development of each plan is a complex and multilayered process with several key stakeholders involved, the most important of which are the Prime Minister's Office, the Ministry of Health and the Ministry of Planning and Finance. The 2010–2015 plan underwent four complete revisions with drafts three and four undergoing independent review, prior to release. The 2010–2015 health plan development and review schedule was as follows [1]:

- June 2009 – An order was received through Circular No. 751 from the Prime Minister to develop the plan. Outcome: The Department of Planning and Finance (DPF) was designated to co-ordinate the development of the plan.
- January 2010 – The DPF established a collaborative team with members from the DPF, Joint Assessment Health Reports (JAHR) representatives, European Committee consultants and WHO Development Partner Coordinators. The team met on a weekly basis. Outcome: A detailed outline of the next plan was drafted.
- January–March 2010 – A situation assessment was conducted through consultations with a wide range of groups including MOH departments, the HPG, universities, research institutions, civil societies and related ministries such as Ministry of Planning and Investment, Ministry of Finance and Ministry of Labour, Invalids and Social Affairs and also referenced reports on previous assessments of the health landscape and previous outcomes of plans. Outcome: A first draft of the plan was produced at the end of March.
- March–June 2010 – The first draft of the plan was sent out to three regions for consultation and Provincial Health Departments in particular were asked for comments and to share their own 5-year plans. All input was considered in meetings between the MOH and the HPG. Outcome: A second draft was released in June.
- June–October 2010 – The JANS tools and WHO six building blocks of health systems were referenced for the first time to self-assess the quality of the plan draft. Outcome: The third draft was released in mid-October.
- October 2010 – Input was sought from the JANS team and the HPG and a full quality assessment was conducted. Outcome: A preliminary quality assessment report with recommendations was released at the end of October.
- November 2010 – The DPF revised the draft based upon recommendations received. Outcome: The final draft was released on November 9 and the official plan published in late December.

This timeline shows that the 2010–2015 health plan took 11 months' work by a wide range of collaborators from local health representatives to global health-focused organisations. The plan was also independently assessed and scrutinised and recommendations were considered and integrated into the final product in an open and transparent way. The plan is therefore broadly accepted and forms the framework for all health-related initiatives for the following 5 years. Interestingly, although the plan is named 2010–2015, it is not actually released until the end of the first year and logically should be 2011–2015. The next plan will commence this cycle in mid-2015.

Primary players throughout this process are the JANS team and the HPG as discussed in Sect. 5.1 but their work does not cease when the plan is signed into operation. Following the release of any health plan, there are two comprehensive assessments. There is a retrospective review of the outcomes and achievements of the previous plan and an evaluation of the quality of the new plan and the developmental methodology used. Both of these reviews are independent and whilst driven by JANS or the HPG, they incorporate ministry, academic, practitioner and international members.

The release of any 5-year plan final version triggers a formal process of independent audit by the JANS team that aims to assess the quality of both the process of developing the plan and the contents of the plan. The assessment extends to cover the implementation, or intended implementation, of the plan through national and provincial health plans.

Each audit is governed and guided by five dimensions (agreed standards) which are further divided into 21 attributes as follows [1]:

- **Dimension 1.** Situation analysis and programming: it seeks to assess the soundness of analysis/assessment underlying identification of the programming contained in the national strategy.
  - Attributes:

    Attribute 1: National strategy is based on a sound situational and response analysis of the context (including political, social, cultural, gender, epidemiological, legal and institutional determinants).

    Attribute 2: Clearly defined priority areas, goals, objectives, interventions and expected outcomes/products that contribute to improving health outcomes and meeting national and global commitments (such as the Millennium Development Goals).

    Attribute 3: Planned interventions are feasible, locally appropriate, equitable and based on evidence and good practice, including consideration of effectiveness and sustainability (both financial and programmatic).

    Attribute 4: Both assessment of risks (analysing feasibility of and potential obstacles to implementation) and proposed mitigation strategies (including specifying technical assistance needs) are present and credible.

- **Dimension 2.** Process: it seeks to assess the soundness and inclusiveness of development and endorsement processes for the national strategy.
  - Attributes:

    Attribute 5: Multi-stakeholder (including government) involvement in development of national strategy and operational plans (led by government, with a transparent participative process) and multi-stakeholder final endorsement

    Attribute 6: High level of political commitment to national strategy

    Attribute 7: National strategy consistent with relevant higher- and/or lower-level strategies, financing frameworks and underlying operational plans

- **Dimension 3.** Finance and auditing: it seeks to assess the soundness of financial and auditing framework and systems.
  - Attributes:

    Attribute 8: Expenditure framework with comprehensive budget/costing of the programme areas covered by the national strategy.

Attribute 9: Expenditure framework includes financial gap analysis – including a specification of known financial pledges against the budget from key domestic and international funding sources.

Attribute 10: Description of financial management system (including financial reporting against budgeted costs and accounting policies and processes) and evidence that it is adequate, accountable and transparent.

Attribute 11: Description of audit procedures and evidence of appropriate scope of audit work, as well as independence and capacity of auditors.

Attribute 12: In the context of national development policies (where applicable): explanation of how external resources will be channelled, managed and reported on, description of relevant domestic financing policies (in relation to different approaches to resource pooling) and if relevant, description of how fiscal space constraints to scaling up spending will be managed.

- **Dimension 4.** Implementation and management: it seeks to assess the soundness of arrangements and systems for implementing and managing the programmes contained in the national strategy.

  - Attributes:

    Attribute 13: Operational plans are regularly developed through a participatory process and detail how strategic plan objectives will be achieved.

    Attribute 14: Description of how resources will be deployed to achieve clearly defined outcomes (with attention to staffing, procurement, logistics and distribution. Plan describes transfer of resources to sub-national level and non-state actors).

    Attribute 15: Procurement policy that complies with international guidelines and evidence of adequate, accountable, and transparent procurement and supply management systems with capacity to reach target populations.

    Attribute 16: Specification of governance, management and co-ordination mechanisms/framework for implementation (roles, responsibilities and decision-making of all stakeholders).

- **Dimension 5.** Results, monitoring and review: soundness of review and evaluation mechanisms and how their results are used.

  - Attributes:

    Attribute 17: Plan for monitoring and evaluation that includes clearly described output and outcome/impact indicators, with related multiyear targets that can be used to measure progress and make performance-based decisions.

    Attribute 18: Plan for monitoring and evaluation includes sources of information for indicators and description of information flows.

Attribute 19: Plan for monitoring and evaluation that includes descriptions of data collection/data management methods, tools and analytical processes (including quality assurance).

Attribute 20: There is a plan for joint periodic performance reviews (reporting of results against specified objectives and respective targets explaining any deviations) and processes for the development of related corrective measures.

Attribute 21: Monitoring and evaluation plan describes processes by which monitoring results can influence decision-making (including financial disbursement).

Each of the five main pillars in the health plan has aspects that have been identified as underperforming against the audit criteria. The detailed results of the 2010–2015 plan audit by the JANS team are provided in Appendix C. Following are the high-level areas of ongoing concern [1, 6].

- Care pathways, standard treatment protocols and practice guidelines are not sufficiently documented, consistent or enforced. This lack of standardised guidance and oversight results in overcrowded specialist facilities, underutilised primary health centres, late referrals for specialist consultation and treatment and performance of unnecessary medical procedures.
- There is ineffective continuum of care and inadequate patient information technology management. As patients advance though treatment levels, undergo referrals or change health facilities, they endure additional costs associated with duplicated procedures because of undefined national standards and lack of information flows between providers and facilities.
- The disparate distribution of qualified medical professional staff affects quality and access to health services in rural and remote locations in particular where service provision is well below demand. This is exacerbated through weak regulatory measures, poor incentives, lack of co-ordination in human resource allocation and management across ministries, poor workforce data, low salaries and a recent overemphasis on technical rather than clinical skills development. The master plan focuses on training individuals without understanding or addressing systemic and endemic workforce issues.
- There is poor inter-ministerial collaboration resulting in fragmented policies and a lack of insight into whole of government issues or opportunities for improvement.
- There is a need to review and strengthen pre-service education. There should be a focus on broadening healthcare professional training and education in line with developing trends in the healthcare landscape and to expand preclinical and in practice capacity building beyond medical doctors to nurses, pharmacists, etc. There should also be greater integration of emerging health fields such as community care, palliative counselling and support and psychosocial professions into training activities.

5.3.2 *Outcomes from Previous Strategic Plans*

There are two important retrospective reviews conducted of previous health plan outcomes and achievements. One is produced by the JANS group and is of relatively high level, the other is by the Joint Annual Health Review (JAHR) to report on more detailed outcomes and provide an assessment of the previous health plan. The JAHR review is annual and is performed collaboratively by the Ministry of Health and the Health Partnership Group. The review is supported by funding for technical and financial assistance from the Health Partnership Group (HPG) and financial support from the WHO, Atlantic Philanthropies, AusAID and USAID/PEPFAR. Whilst these reviews are conducted on an annual basis, the one immediately following a new 5-year plan is particularly important as it provides a detailed retrospective review of the previous plan and recommendations for the future strategic direction, together with an update on current health trends and status and an analysis of health financing and health system governance. These recommendations are integrated into the long-term vision which is bound and enforced by the legal framework.

The JANS review audits achievements stated in national government reporting against the eight Millennium Development Goals (MDG). The most recent of the JAHR reviews was the December 2011 review. This review concluded that the Vietnamese health sector as a whole was on track to achieve all goals by 2015. Whilst overall the outcomes look positive, there was however an identified disparity between urban and rural areas and the gap was largest in remote areas. Following are their reported outcomes following assessment against the MDG [1] (Table 5.1).

Each annual review provides recommendations for implementation of the strategies in the 5-year plan but cannot influence any change in strategy between plans. Most importantly they also provide solutions to the issues and a long- and short-term action plan with targets and measures to measure against. The annual reviews are highly detailed and provide important information regarding progress and trends to assist with planning and decision-making at the provincial level for the coming year. The following recommendations were provided as a result of the 2011 review:

Table 5.1 Progress by MDG in accordance with national government reporting

MDG1	Eradicate extreme poverty and hunger	Achieved
MDG2	Achieve universal primary education	Very likely to be achieved, on track
MDG3	Promote gender equality and empower women	Very likely to be achieved, on track
MDG4	Reduce child mortality	Very likely to be achieved, on track
MDG5	Improve maternal health	Very likely to be achieved, on track
MDG6	Combat HIV/AIDS, malaria and other diseases	Possible to achieve if some changes are made
MDG7	Ensure environmental sustainability	Very likely to be achieved, on track
MDG8	Develop a global partnership for development	Insufficient information

Table 5.2 identifies a number of key areas for attention and presents, as yet, unimplemented solutions. It also demonstrates that although the plan covers abroad range of health issues and aims to address some significant areas of need, there are gaps between strategy, policy and implementation. Intention does not result in improvement without action but a key barrier to achieving the intentions is a lack of capacity and skills. Given this lack of appropriate manpower, it is also very difficult to cover such a broad range of projects and national programmes at the same time. This lack of capacity often means that there is, at best, only minimal measured achievement possible in any area. Over time it can appear that much is planned but little change is seen at the grass-roots level leaving feelings of disenfranchisement by all.

5.3.3 Strategic Objectives

The JANS and JAHR reviews provide valuable independent insight into the state of the Vietnamese health sector and their recommendations highlight areas of concern that should be applied to identify and influence future strategic programme development and investment. As noted in the previous section, it is not possible to sustain or give traction to projects across all areas of the health landscape at once and the reviews should be used to evidence priorities. These priority areas could be either selected based on those which have already seen some improvement and hence have support and momentum or those where there is appropriate international interest and hence can incorporate capacity building with lowered financial investment. There is overlap between the JANS and JAHR reports as would be expected. The following common foci have been identified for primary attention in the next strategic health plan [1, 6]:

Child and Maternal Health
There is significant disparity in child mortality across Viet Nam and the rates are significantly poorer among ethnic minorities, the very poor and those living in remote areas. These three characteristics often coexist in single population groups requiring any solution to be multifaceted and collaborative across a number of ministries.

A high prevalence of stunting in young children remains evident and is closely linked to the low rate of exclusive breastfeeding in some areas and the implementation of the global code on marketing breast milk substitute. Unfortunately the trends of the west are being replayed in Viet Nam but this presents an opportunity to turn the tide through education and community care in particular without having to devise unique solutions. This enables tried and tested programmes to be ready to pilot within a short time frame after some degree of contextualisation rather than designing and developing from a blank page.

TB, Malaria and HIV/AIDS There is a need to improve capacity in laboratory infrastructure and resourcing and procurement of best-practice medications to

Table 5.2 Issues and solutions from JAHR 2012 report

Pillar	Issue	Solution
Human resources:	Health workforce is not distributed evenly across regions	Continue to develop policies with an appropriate priority on disadvantaged regions and fields lacking health workers like tuberculosis, leprosy, mental health
Develop a health manpower adequate in numbers and structure and with a more balanced distribution	Inappropriate policies for using, recruiting health workers (low income)	Study a model for using health workers that is appropriate for disadvantaged regions
Quality of health worker training and education does not yet meet requirements	Apparent shift in health workforce from mountainous to delta areas, from lower levels to higher levels, from preventive to curative care	Improve the health manpower information system (including private sector health workers)
	Shortage of health workers for certain specialisations like TB, leprosy, mental health, preventive medicine because of low income, and poor working conditions	Assess effectiveness of various forms of training used in recent years, especially related to the goal of providing health workers to mountainous, remote, isolated regions, lower-level facilities. Based on results of the assessment, make appropriate adjustments
	The education accreditation system lacks indicators specific to medical training	Improve quality of training and ensure performance of health workers
	There is a lack of regulations on training, retraining for health workers to satisfy requirements of the law on examination and treatment	Develop a comprehensive long-term plan for reforming medical training for the entire medical training system
	Many retraining courses lack trainees because health facilities are short of staff and some health workers don't want to go for training far from home	Develop criteria for accreditation specific to training in health science fields and apply this in the general education quality accreditation system
	Competency standards for each type of health worker are not yet in place to serve as a standard for outputs of the training system. learning, e-learning and methods appropriate for health workers in disadvantaged regions	Develop a long-term comprehensive plan and regulations on retraining and continuing medical education to meet the requirements for updating knowledge of health workers
		Diversify forms of retraining, capacity strengthening for health workers, paying special attention to distance
		Develop competency standards for each type of health worker

Finance and infrastructure:	Macroeconomic difficulties led to tightening of the state budget, reduction in public spending and limitations in issuing government bonds	Develop and implement a midterm expenditure plan for the coming period
State budget spending on health should reach 10 % of total state budget spending	There are not yet guidelines for allocating state budget based on performance and output indicators	Reform the mechanism for allocating state budget to health facilities based on performance and output indicators
	A regulatory impact assessment has not been implemented on the proposed decree reforming the operational and financial mechanisms applied to state health service facilities	The Ministry of Health should issue guidelines for allocating state budget based on performance and output indicators
	Some socio-economic environment conditions and health sector factors are not yet appropriate for implementing autonomy in state health facilities	Reform the operational mechanism, especially the financing mechanism of public health facilities, towards autonomy with transparency and openness
	Monitoring, checking on autonomous activities has not yet been implemented due to limitations in manpower and instruments	There is a need to implement a regulatory impact assessment of the proposed decree on reforming the operational and financial mechanisms of state health facilities
	There is not yet effective control over prescription of pharmaceuticals and diagnostics	Develop an internally consistent policy and harmonise the process of autonomisation in the health sector with external factors
	There is a lack of information on cost-effectiveness of medical interventions	Strengthen capacity for state management in implementation of autonomy in state health facilities
	There is not yet a complete assessment of malfeasance in the health sector	Strengthen effectiveness in use of existing financial resources
	Out-of-pocket spending on health remains at high levels compared to the WHO recommendation (30 % of total health spending)	Strengthen control to ensure rational prescription of pharmaceuticals, diagnostic services based on practice guidelines
	The proportion of households facing catastrophic health spending remains high and has not fallen over time	Strongly promote use of information on cost-effectiveness in deciding on medical interventions

(continued)

Table 5.2 (continued)

Pillar	Issue	Solution
	Fee for service remains the primary mechanism for provider payments and is causing many abuses	There is a need for a rigorous assessment of malfeasance in the health sector with proposals for appropriate anti-corruption measures
		Control healthcare costs, reduce gradually the share of total health spending that comes directly from out-of-pocket spending of the people
		There is a need to speed up the development of standard treatment guidelines for common medical conditions. A regular and effective mechanism for monitoring of pharmaceutical and medical service prices needs to be set up
		Develop a plan and road map for reforming hospital payments
Pharmaceuticals, medical equipment and infrastructure	Antibiotic use in hospitals, the community and in livestock raising has not yet been supervised	Strengthen appropriate use of antibiotics. Set up a surveillance network on antibiotic use in hospitals and in the community
	Some measures for controlling drug prices have not yet been incorporated into policies or revised in a timely fashion	Collaborate with the Ministry of Agriculture and Rural Development for supervision of antibiotic use in livestock and poultry raising and aquaculture
	Many regulations related to use and circulation of pharmaceuticals have not yet been implemented	Establish a pharmaceutical price control mechanism with the participation of agencies inside and outside the health sector
	There is a lack of concern about the most basic equipment needs at the grass-roots level	Supplement and complete mechanisms for pharmaceutical price controls (such as competitive bidding procedures, regulations capping wholesale margins, etc. for essential drugs and a mechanism of administrative penalties for violations)
	State budget (local and central) does not meet the rapidly growing need for medical infrastructure	Determine essential drugs and propose that the state support prices when market prices fluctuate widely
		Impose severe penalties for violations of existing regulations, for example, the prescription drug regulations
		Invest in appropriate technology for each level
		Update the essential medical equipment lists for different level facilities
		Promote basic investments in health facilities
		Increase social resources invested in medical infrastructure

Health information:	Plans for development of the health information system have still not been issued	Develop and finalise policies on health management information systems to create effective conditions to satisfy the need for a legal framework for both the public and private health sectors in relation to provision of health information data
Finalise policies, plans for development of the health information system	Regulations have not yet been developed on collaboration and information sharing within the health sector and with other relevant ministries	Develop and implement legal documents regulating organisation of manpower, budget for statistical activities at all levels, with clear stipulations of the functions and responsibility of the leaders, statistical workers from the central, provincial, district to the commune levels
Strengthen capacity to meet the needs of data users	There is a lack of documents regulating responsibilities and obligations for updating information, reporting data on health service provision activities of private medical and pharmaceutical facilities	Review and revise the system of indicators, registers, health statistic reports, guidelines on health management information, hospital information, preventive medicine information and control of epidemics, information related to teaching and research. Decentralise responsibility for the indicator system to each level. Develop an indicator dictionary
Improve provision of information, analysis and use of statistical data	The systems of indicators, registers and statistical reports, guiding documents on the health management information system, hospital, preventive medicine and disease control information have not been finalised	Close cooperation is needed on collection, processing, provision and sharing of information within the Ministry of Health and with related ministries and agencies like the General Statistical Office, Ministry of Finance, Ministry of Justice, General Administration of Population and Family Planning, VSS and other sectors
	Statistical data quality has not yet been evaluated according to 6 criteria of quality (relevance, accuracy, timeliness, accessibility, comparability and coherence)	Improve dissemination of information in different and diverse forms appropriate for data users
	Information in some areas is still lacking, for example, on the private health sector, cause of death, risk factors for non-communicable diseases and activities of state health facilities	Develop a centre for integration of health information data to ensure unified, concentrated management with one focal point, allocate responsibility for data collection and data sharing

(continued)

Table 5.2 (continued)

Pillar	Issue	Solution
	Non-communicable disease registration and death registration in the community have not yet been strengthened	Gradually modernise the health information system appropriate with financial, technical ability and with the data needs of different levels of the health system, including activities to upgrade, develop and apply software for management, processing, transmitting and archiving information, ensure that all levels can process relevant reports
	A proposal to mobilise funds to implement a second National Health Survey has not yet been developed	Organise an in-depth and comprehensive assessment of the periodic reporting system to identify aspects that are acceptable and difficulties that need to be resolved, whilst at the same time put in place sanctions for administrative violations in statistics
	Clear and concrete health information dissemination and sharing policies have not yet been developed, statistical data are disseminated quite late limiting their usefulness	Develop a mechanism and create resources to strengthen dissemination and sharing of health information through many different channels
	The Health Statistics Yearbook has not yet been put on the Internet, is slow to be printed each year compared to the needs of users	
	The ability to analyse and use data has not yet been adequately strengthened. Statistical data are only analysed at a basic level, with simple information products, but in-depth analysis and use of health statistics data for planning and policymaking remains limited	
	Many information sources lack a mechanism for dissemination, release of data making them difficult to access; knowledge on use of data for analysis, evaluation, forecasting by public managers, planners and statisticians at all levels remains limited; database archives at all levels are weak, do not include relevant data from alternative sources; data are not managed in a scientific manner and are slow to apply modern technologies for updating, archiving and transmitting data	

Primary healthcare, preventive medicine and national health target programmes:	Shortage of professional staff	Strengthen short- and long-term training of young health workers for specialisation in preventive medicine
Prevent major outbreak, cope with newly emerging diseases	Few professional staff have experience, excellent professional skills and effective training	Open training courses for grass-roots health workers when programmes/projects are implemented
Control of HIV/AIDS, tuberculosis, leprosy, malaria, dengue fever and other communicable diseases	Monitoring, surveillance, disease control at the commune and district levels is weak	Consolidate activities of the commune health station. Implement new benchmarks for commune healthcare
Expanded programme on immunisation	Outbreaks of dengue fever, hand-foot-and-mouth disease have occurred in many southern localities	Strengthen support, supervision from higher level facilities in all areas of preventive medicine for lower-level facilities
Improve food quality and ensure food safety and hygiene	Awareness of disease prevention and control among the population and local grass-roots level authorities in many places remains low	Fully implement the health professional remuneration policy for preventive medicine workers issued by the government
Manage the health environment, control risk factors to health due to pollution, unhealthy lifestyles	Risk of mother-to-child transmission of HIV/AIDS has not been adequately controlled	Strengthen IEC and policy advocacy at the grass-roots level
Complete the model of organisation and consolidate the grass-roots health network	Provision of ARV treatment remains limited	Strengthen the amount and quality of health IEC related to HIV/AIDS control and other dangerous communicable diseases at the central and local levels
Strengthen health IEC	Multiple drug-resistant TB is being detected	Diversify messages and forms of IEC so target audiences can absorb the knowledge and change behaviour
	Dengue fever remains widespread (nearly 100, 000 people infected)	Consolidate the commune and village health networks, maintain effective operations
	Few grass-roots health workers have received training in the expanded programme on immunisations, with clear consequences for quality of vaccination services	Strengthen support, supervision and early detection of epidemic diseases
	Increasing trend in sexual transmission of HIV infection	Continue to supplement, complete legal documents on food safety and hygiene to clarify responsibilities for implementation
	Stigmatisation of people living with HIV/AIDS has not been eradicated	Continue to invest in human resource training, equipment, infrastructure for food hygiene and safety work at the central, provincial and district levels

(continued)

Table 5.2 (continued)

Pillar	Issue	Solution
	The health sector has only recently been given responsibility to serve as the focal point to ensure food safety; inter-sectoral cooperation has only begun to be improved	Strengthen and increase the number and quality of food safety inspections of food processing facilities, communal eating halls, public eating facilities
		Promote health IEC on food hygiene and safety in the community, in schools, in enterprises and in the mass media
	Physical facilities, equipment, financial and human resources in the health sector for food hygiene and safety remains weak at the provincial and district levels	National plan for control of non-communicable diseases
	Habits of the people in production, buying, selling, processing and using unhygienic foods have not improved much over time	Promote health IEC to improve awareness and practice of community leadership on health and environmental protection and developing healthy lifestyles
	Checking, inspection, surveillance of food hygiene and safety are not yet widely implemented, especially in small-scale food production and distribution facilities, in traditional markets and in rural areas	Implement national health target programmes and projects in all localities including preventive programmes
	Large-scale food poisoning incidents are still occurring, especially in industrial zones	Policy advocacy so the national assembly passes the law on tobacco control in the first quarter of 2012
	Environmental pollution is increasing as levels of industrialisation, urbanisation and population increase	Tighten inter-sectoral collaboration to jointly resolve health problems requiring actions from multiple ministries and agencies
	Activities in treatment of medical waste, labour hygiene and safety, control of accidents and injuries, school health, healthcare of the elderly have only begun to see some initial successes	Strengthen international cooperation to take advantage of technical support, international experts and financial support in all preventive medicine programmes and disease

	Many weaknesses remain and there is a lack of necessary resources. Inter-sectoral cooperation remains weak at many levels in some areas of public health (accidents, injuries, occupational health, domestic violence, tobacco control and harm reduction related to alcohol use)	Implement early and widely the national standards for preventive medicine following guidelines of the Ministry of Health
	The grass-roots health system faces many pressures of a high workload but inadequate investments in professional training, physical facilities, equipment, financing and personnel policy	Strengthen provincial-level support and supervision of preventive medicine, primary healthcare and national health target programme/project activities at the district and commune levels
	Guidance for the grass-roots level from many different departments and administrations of the Ministry of Health requires better co-ordination, integration	Continue to collaborate with communication agencies, television, radio, newspapers at the central and local levels, increase the frequency and quality of health protection and disease control information products
	Awareness about protection, care and promotion of the people's health remains limited. Harmful behaviour remains common	Encourage and support various forms of popular culture, performances with topics on preventive medicine in the community
	People implementing health IEC often lack professional training	Encourage and support the establishment and activities of health clubs for different demographic groups in the community
	IEC channels, forms and messages are not yet diverse, active, attractive	
	Campaigns to increase physical exercise for health protection have not been widely developed or implemented in the community	
Examination and treatment:	The district health system model has not yet been unified	Continue to assess implementation of Circular No. 3 to achieve a unified organisational model at the district level
Access and equity	Overcrowding remains prevalent in central, provincial and some specialised hospitals	Create convenience and ensure rights of insured patients
Improve quality of examination and treatment services	There is not yet a system of quality management in the health sector	Implement congruent policies in the short- and long-term to overcome hospital overcrowding

(continued)

Table 5.2 (continued)

Pillar	Issue	Solution
Improve management capacity, strengthen effectiveness of medical examination and treatment	Awareness of health sector managers about service quality management remains limited	Standardise quality of health services, hospital quality, gradually meet regional and international standards
Resolve overcrowded hospitals	Little attention has been paid to service quality to ensure patient satisfaction	Implement provision of curative care services according to an adjusted referral system, improve procedures for providing medical services to insured patients
	Referrals, administrative procedures, health insurance reimbursements remain complicated and difficult	Set up a quality management system for examination and treatment at the Ministry of Healthprovincial health bureaus and at medical facilities after issuing a circular guiding implementation of hospital quality management
	Quality assurance models and methods are only implemented in a few hospitals	Promote the setting up of an organisation to certify quality
	Salary and salary supplements do not provide health workers with appropriate levels of remuneration commensurate with the human capital and risks involved in health sector work	Recognise selected foreign hospital quality standard systems
	Market mechanisms are negatively affecting health worker behaviour	Strengthen advocacy, awareness raising, training on quality management in the health sector
	There are a large number of professional, treatment and technical procedure guidelines and care pathways, with few resources for their implementation	Implement quality methods in medical facilities
	Decrees, circulars guiding issuing of practice licences, permits have not yet been approved	Improve medical ethics
	The user fee schedule is outdated and no longer appropriate, it does not ensure recovery of the costs of providing examination and treatment services	Find a policy mechanism to improve salaries, income of public sector health workers

	Autonomisation is causing hardship in reducing hospital overcrowding at higher levels and creates the risk of overprescription of pharmaceuticals, diagnostic and other technical services	Strengthen checking and supervision of compliance with the law on examination and treatment and the statement of conduct in the health sector
	Health technology assessment has not yet been implemented, there is no experience to do so	Supplement and/or update professional guidelines focused on common techniques, common diseases, widely used techniques
	Some problems have resulted from implementing joint ventures, partnerships, capital contributions to invest in hospital equipment	Pilot assessment of implementation for professional guidelines
		Complete the practice registration system
		Implement practice licencing following the road map
		Set up a system to register practitioners to support management of medical practitioners
		Strengthen training to continuously update knowledge
		Reform the operational mechanism and financial mechanism of state health facilities towards greater autonomy, transparency and openness
		Supplement and revise the user fee schedule based on full costing that ensures the operation and development of the hospital
		Reform the mechanism for state budget allocation and provider payments for curative care
		Implement methods to control hospital costs
		Implement health technology assessment in order to control and eliminate use of ineffective technologies, drugs, techniques
		Pilot health technology assessment
		Evaluate and develop solutions to mobilise an appropriate level of social resources
		Continue to evaluate all private sector participation in investments in state medical facilities to develop appropriate forms

(continued)

Table 5.2 (continued)

Pillar	Issue	Solution
Family planning, fertility and reproductive health:	28 out of 63 provinces have not yet reached replacement fertility, and others have seen an increase in fertility rate	Develop and implement projects to address the national strategy on population and reproductive health
Maintain replacement fertility (TFR below 2.1)	Sex ratio at birth is increasing rapidly	Strengthen leadership to implement Resolution No. 47-NQ/TW on population and family planning
Ensure appropriate sex balance	Population quality is slow to be ameliorated	Develop action plan on population and reproductive health
Improve population quality	Health indicators of mothers and children in disadvantaged and mountainous regions show wide disparities compared to delta areas	Reduce the child malnutrition rate
	Reproductive tract infections and sexually transmitted diseases remain widespread	The Ministry of Health should complete the national nutrition strategy and submit it to the government for approval as soon as practical
	Screening for early detection of reproductive tract cancers has not yet been widely implemented	Improve the quality of reproductive health services including family planning
	Reproductive health of specific target groups: youth, the disabled, the elderly, people in disadvantaged regions, has not been paid adequate attention and lacks resources	
	The risk of a double burden of malnutrition, undernutrition, and overnutrition, obesity	

address multiple drug-resistant (MDR) and in particular extensively drug-resistant (XDR) TB. Both forms of resistance are reported in Viet Nam.

The incidence of these conditions is reducing but the focus is now turning to early case detection and appropriate treatment to prevent secondary multiple drug-resistant tuberculosis. Although there are many projects in this space, there is a culture change required both in the general population and in medical professionals especially at the onset of symptoms.

Capacity Building Building the capacity of the local healthcare platform both through human resource development and technology and laboratory strengthening is constantly documented as issues within the Vietnamese health system. Most large-scale research or clinical projects incorporate some level of capacity building but large-scale improvement requires a national approach and should begin at university for all medical students rather than taking a fragmented, reactive approach. There is again a multifaceted approach required as both quality and quantity need to be improved and exposure to emerging conditions, best-practice management of NCDs, health technologies and health management frameworks also need to be addressed.

The government is striving to develop and consolidate local pharmaceutical manufacturing and testing services and these audits support that strategic direction. Sustained international support will however be required if ISOs are to be implemented and local managers, technicians and clinicians are to be enabled to sustain the industry into the future. This is clearly a long-term proposition.

Social and Lifestyle The audits have also recently identified a number of lifestyle predicated health risks. Tobacco use and alcohol have been part of the lifestyle of many Vietnamese for a long time; however, both of these, together with the associated health effects, are seeing increased incidence across both sexes and all ages. There is also frequent mention of NCDs increasing, especially those related to stress and the rapid introduction of western diets. NCDs will focus prominently in the next health plan and in other areas of government policymaking as suggested below.

In the News [17] The Ministry of Health has proposed to raise the tax rates on tobacco to 105 % in 2015 and 145 % in 2018 and health warnings will be provided by pictures on tobacco packages. The Ministry of Finance is about to submit the draft amendments to the Law on Luxury Tax to the National Assembly, including tobacco products. Accordingly, the Government proposed the luxury tax rate on cigarettes to be 70 % for the period from 1/1/2016 to 31/1/2018 and 75 % from 01/01/2019. The rates are lower than originally proposed by the Ministry of Finance, up by only 5 % for the 2016–2018 period, and the starting time is also later. Based on this proposal, the increase of cigarette prices in 3 years to 2018 would be 2.9 % or under 1 % a year while Vietnam's GDP growth is forecast to be more than 5 %/year during this time.

'This means that the real increase of tobacco prices is lower than the growth rate of GDP, so the purchasing power of tobacco will still increase. Such an increase is too low. The goal of raising tobacco taxes to reduce cigarette consumption will not be achieved', said Ms. Pham Thi Hoang Anh, Director of HealthBridge Canada in Viet Nam.

This is the third time that tobacco taxes have been adjusted in the last 10 years. Luong Ngoc Khue, a senior official from the Ministry of Health, said that it was necessary to learn from experience from the increase of tobacco taxes in 2006 and 2008.

In 2006, the luxury tax rates on tobacco products of 25 %, 45 % and 65 % were given the common rate of 55 %. Since 2008, this rate has increased by 10 %. As a result, the real price of cigarettes actually rose in the first tax hike and fell in the following hike. 'The increase in luxury tax of 10 % in 2008 does not guarantee a reduction of tobacco consumption in the long term. That means the proposed tax increase of only 5 % will not be able to help reduce tobacco consumption as expected', said Khue.

The Ministry of Health proposed two options. Firstly, in order to achieve the national target in reducing tobacco consumption, in 2015 the luxury tax rate will be 105 % and in 2018 145 %. This is considered the optimal increase. Secondly, to keep the purchasing power of tobacco constant, the adjusted tax rate should be 85 % by 2015 and 105 % by 2018.

With the second option, the increase of retail prices is close to the actual income growth. It is estimated that the smoking rate for men must fall from 47.4 % in 2014 to 42.1 % in 2020 to achieve nearly two-thirds of the target set in the National Strategy for Prevention of Adverse Effects of Cigarettes to 2020. In fact, even in a difficult economic context, the performance of the tobacco industry is still very good. As reported by the Viet Nam Tobacco Corporation in 2013, the consumption of cigarettes was more than 102 % of the annual plan, up 7.7 %.

Lessons learned from Thailand show that regular tobacco tax increase is a win-win policy and does not affect the tobacco industry. From 1994 to 2012, the Thai government raised the luxury tax on tobacco ten times. Thus, the price of cigarettes increased from 15 Bath/pack to 65 Bath/bag and the smoking rates among men decreased from 59 % in 1991 to less than 42 % in 2011.

Tobacco smoke contains over 7000 chemicals, including 70 carcinogens. Tobacco use causes 25 diseases such as lung cancer, laryngeal cancer, oral cavity cancer, skin cancer, heart disease and others. Smoking causes 90 % of lung cancer cases, 75 % of chronic obstructive pulmonary disease cases and 25 % of ischemic heart disease cases.

About 100 million people died from diseases related to tobacco use around the world in the twentieth century. Each year tobacco causes nearly six million deaths and the number is predicted to increase to more than eight million people in 2020. Le Ha.

5.4 Opportunities and Barriers to Effective Healthcare Management

> Access to service is affected by geographical, financial, and cultural factors, a challenge heightened by an outdated national certification system for health providers and disparities in medical human resources. Health education and communication campaigns have not effectively targeted the beneficiaries. [18]

The JAHR has both identified problems to be addressed in upcoming years and evidenced that current projects are have not appropriately designed and/or implemented to achieve the stated aims. This means that whilst much work would appear to be being done, many of the same issues appear in each plan as targets are not being met. There are several barriers preventing progress and these have been discussed throughout this book. For real change to be effected and sustained, there is a need for culture change both in the general population and in practice communities. Medical education needs to be made relevant for modern Viet Nam and needs to be assessed against international standards for general and medical higher education.

There is an identified need to develop an analytical, evidence-based approach to health planning, strategy development and policymaking. This will ensure that upcoming trends are being identified, managed, monitored and addressed before they become a huge burden on society and the nation's finance systems. However, again this is not as simple as it sounds in a country that does not have an integrated technology platform for health and does not cultivate the required statistical and informatics skills in its health programmes at universities. It is also difficult in an environment where there is a large and wide-ranging group of stakeholders involved in each decision, each of which has their own agenda and none of which want to relinquish any control or funding opportunities.

The following issues have been priorities for a number of years and are expected to remain so for several more given their continued listing in audit recommendations [1, 6, 19]. For international researchers and organisations, they present yet more opportunities to solve real, long-term healthcare problems for Viet Nam.

- Relatively large disparities in health status across regions and income groups.
- Changing disease patterns, people's growing need for healthcare and increasing adverse risk factors to health need to be addressed.
- Grass-roots healthcare networks face huge difficulties, especially in mountainous, remote and isolated areas and preventive medicine networks remain weak.
- Inter-sectoral collaboration and public participation in preventive work is limited. Understanding and awareness on health protection and promotion is weak.
- The responsiveness of the curative care network is limited. Quality of care and hospital overcrowding and financial management remain problems.

For real change to be realised in Viet Nam, it is clear that a multifaceted approach is required. This approach must include consideration of financial, human resource, cultural, clinical, organisational, management and compliance factors. Whilst progress has been measured, it is fragmented and too often does not serve those it aimed to serve and does not achieve the strategic goals set. One key problem is that policies are developed and implemented in isolation without full support (or knowledge) of all stakeholders. The stakeholders that feel excluded then erect new barriers and this is especially relevant where funding is available but is monopolised by one group or ministerial department, even though collaborators may be required for implementation.

A key recommendation for future policy reform would be to undertake a full evaluation of the environment incorporating a maturity assessment, gap analysis, change management and operational architecture mapping to enable national planning in an informed environment where risk management can be undertaken, any ramifications to change can be identified and managed proactively and outcomes can be assessed, measured and reported. There should also be more public transparency within reform programmes to enable a more accurate understanding of the true state of healthcare quality and processes to be gained and socialised not only in Viet Nam but around the world. There would appear to be a real need to step back and revise the whole political reform process in Viet Nam. Whilst radical, an overhaul will facilitate more comprehensive strategic programmes underpinned by stronger policies that will systematically reduce the healthcare mythology that currently exists and allow an evidence-based wisdom to evolve. This does not however mean that the political structures or foundations need to change, only the processes within them that allow the ideals to be effected.

References

1. Nguyen VT, Ha DA, Tran MO, Prakongsai P, Tangcharoensathien V (2011) The independent assessment of the process and the content of the five year health plan, 2011–15, in Vietnam. Final report 7 January 2011. Ministry of Health of Viet Nam, Health Partnerships Group, Joint Annual Health Review 2011, Hanoi
2. Personal communication Do Dang An. MOH and HRG representative. Received 23 Sept 2014
3. http://hpg.icdmoh.gov.vn/. Accessed 23 Sept 2014
4. www.ngocentre.org.vn/content/membership-information. Accessed 12 Oct 2014
5. VPHA (2013) Annual report 2013. www.vpha.org.vn/component/option,com.../Itemid.../view,category/. Accessed 23 Sept 2014
6. U.S. Government Global Health Initiative Strategy (2011) Vietnam V5.0. Aug 2011
7. Barroy H, Jarawan E, Balesd, S (2014) Universal health coverage for inclusive and sustainable development. Country summary report for Vietnam. World Bank Group. Sept 2014. www.worldbank.org/en/topic/health/brief/uhc-japan. Accessed 10 Oct 2014
8. Marriott A (2011) Vietnam's health care system suffers on policy failure. Global Health Check. Www.globalhealthcheck.org/?p=423. Accessed 19 Aug 2014
9. Minh HV, Bach TX (2013) Assessing the household financial burden associated with the chronic non-communicable diseases in rural district of Vietnam. Glob Health Action 2013 5. doi:10.3402/gha.v5i0.18892. Accessed 5 Dec 2014

10. Business Monitor International (2014) Vietnam pharmaceuticals and health care report Q2 2014. SKU: BMI5225042. www.marketresearch.com/Business-Monitor-International-v304/Vietnam-Pharmaceuticals-healthcare-Q2-8100354/. Accessed 12 Nov 2014
11. Nghiem DT (2010) Social health insurance in Viet Nam. Health Insurance Department, Ministry of Health, Ha Noi, 12 Oct 2010. http://www.ilo.org/wcmsp5/groups/public/---asia/---ro-bangkok/---ilo-hanoi/documents/presentation/wcms_145792.pdf. Accessed 10 Nov 2014
12. USAID (2013) Barriers to access and use of public TB diagnostic services in Vietnam. Report released February 2013. http://www.path.org/publications/detail.php?i=2284. Accessed 26 Aug 2014
13. Tran TV, Hoang TP, Mathauer I, Nguy TKP (2011) A health financing review of Viet Nam with a focus on social health insurance. World Health Organisation. Aug 2011. http://www.who.int/health_financing/documents/oasis_f_11-vietnam.pdf. Accessed 5 Dec 2014
14. Nguyen D, Hoang H, Hoang, VM (2013) Public health in Vietnam: scientific evidence for policy changes and interventions. Editorial. Glob Health Action 2013 6:20443. http://dx.doi.org/10.3402/gha.v610.20443. Accessed 05 Dec 2014
15. Toan DT, Hu W, Thai PQ, Hoat LN, Wright P, Martens P (2013) Hot spot detection and spatio-temporal dispersion of dengue fever in Hanoi, Vietnam. Glob Health Action 2013 6. doi:10.3402/gha.v6i0.18632. Accessed 05 Dec 2014
16. An DTM, Minh HV, Huong LT, Hai PT, Giang KB, Xuan LTT et al (2013) Knowledge of health consequences of tobacco smoking: a cross sectional survey of Vietnamese adults. Glob Health Action. doi:10.3402/gha.v6i0.19707, Accessed Dec 6 2014
17. Ha L (2014) VIETNAMNET VietNamNet Bridge. Health ministry proposes tax hike on tobacco products. Posted on 24 Sept 2014. www.talkvietnam.com/2014/09/health-ministry-proposes-tax-hike-on-tobacco-products/. Accessed 26 Sept 2014
18. Nguyen TKT, Pham TL, Nguyen LH, Pham TT, Bales S (eds) (2012) Joint Annual Health Review. Vietnamese Ministry of Health and Health Partnerships Group, Hanoi
19. United Nations (2011) Viet Nam annual report 2011. May 2011. www.un.org.vn. Accessed 10 Oct 2014

Chapter 6
Health Research

6.1 Overview of Active Research Groups

There is a very wide range of research groups and NGOs operating in Viet Nam, and every major philanthropic organisation has Viet Nam listed as a priority country for funding. A representative overview of organisations and projects is provided in this section. Current and future research projects can be informed by understanding what the current foci are and where the gaps are as compared to the ministerial health plans and review reports on priority areas as discussed in the previous section. There may also be opportunities to engage in collaborative projects and funding proposals by better understanding the research environment and key players in the Vietnamese health context.

The three biggest sources of health research capacity for Viet Nam are the UN, the USA and Australia. The projects are primarily funded by government or philanthropic organisations. The most prominent funding sources are:

- Atlantic Philanthropies
- Bill and Melinda Gates Foundation
- Bixby Foundation
- Fabert Foundation
- Global Fund to Fight AIDS, Tuberculosis and Malaria
- Grand Challenges Canada
- McKnight Foundation
- United States Agency for International Development
- Australian Agency for International Development
- Australian Research Council
- US Biomedical Advanced Research and Department Authority
- United States Department of State
- The World Bank
- The Asian Development Bank
- William and Flora Hewlett Foundation

A.G. Shillabeer, *The Health of Vietnam*, DOI 10.1007/978-981-287-709-3_6

Table 6.1 One Plan Viet Nam expenditure by funding source 2008–2011 (USD) [1]

Funding source	2008	2009	2010	2011
Regular resources	17,229,489	20,412,511	19,354,464	23,047,094
Other resources	41,917,953	38,266,561	43,017,956	42,110,872
One Plan fund	12,360,608	19,651,628	32,639,557	20,996,320
Total	71,508,050	78,330,700	95,011,977	86,154,285

Table 6.2 One Plan expenditure in Viet Nam by UN agency in 2011 (USD) [1]

UN agency	Regular resources in 2011	Other resources in 2011	One Plan fund in 2011	Total expenditure in 2011
FAO	490,341	5,763,922	762,061	7,016,324
ILO	577,209	7,782,906	1,705,662	10,065,777
UNAIDS	117,225	924,848	244,378	1,286,451
UNDP	8,975,510	5,339,224	4,893,451	19,208,185
UNESCO	489,763	486,770	530,485	1,507,018
UNFPA	4,319,087	1,126,989	1,762,972	7,209,048
UN-Habitat	709,662	15,000	261,741	986,403
UNICEF	4,169,946	5,818,503	6,635,501	16,623,950
UNIDO	28,806	5,988,467	1,209,748	7,227,021
UNODC	84,342	1,254,401	1,125,082	2,463,825
UNV	200,858	–	88,203	289,061
UN Women	463,725	368,535	525,033	1,357,293
WHO	2,420,620	7,241,306	1,252,002	10,913,927
Total	23,047,094	42,110,872	20,996,320	86,154,285

The funding amounts provided by these and other smaller providers are significant. The following tables outline research investment to UN agencies by One Plan which is one of the many funding sources from the USA (Tables 6.1 and 6.2).

Health research in Viet Nam is conducted by three main types of entity: universities, aid/NGO entities, and government agencies. The UN agencies, CDC, World Bank, Asian Development Bank and USAID are the major contributors. In 2015, the World Bank alone will be providing over 100 m USD for medical education capacity building. Australia has the following active engagement in a broad range of health projects in 2014 (Table 6.3).

Most research is headed by international organisations, but often with a Vietnamese national or expat as part of the team. This is mainly due to the fact that Vietnamese universities have not developed a research culture, except in small pockets, and there are few English language publications achieved, so Vietnamese-led research is largely hidden. Recent work by the Asian Development Bank and World Bank to integrate world standards into medical higher education will hopefully create a much needed impetus and capacity improvement for local research, but until then it will remain externally driven. To facilitate greater local research, there will need to be intensive mentoring by respected international

Table 6.3 Australian representative health projects

Organisation	Organisation type
Sight for All Foundation	Non-government service organisation
Sydney Nursing School	University
Queensland University of Technology	University
The Boomerang Cleft Care Organisation Australia	Charity and not-for-profit
Fred Hollows Foundation	Charity and not-for-profit
The Global Drowning Fund	Non-government service organisation
Trinh Foundation Australia	Non-government service organisation
University of Melbourne	University
University of Sydney and Children's Hospital	University/hospital
Vic Health Education Team	Not-for-profit organisation
Woolcock Institute of Medical Research	Not-for-profit organisation

academics and a programme to improve and sustain English language skills. Given that international researchers need to understand the local environment and cultural foundations, the local and international needs seem to provide a natural synergy from which both can produce something better than would be possible in isolation. Connecting with local universities would therefore be a constructive first step to facilitate any new research project.

The PATH Story [2–6]

> Path is an international non-profit organisation that transforms global health through innovation. We take an entrepreneurial approach to developing and delivering high-impact, low-cost solutions. [3]

PATH (Program for Alternative Technology in Health until 2014) was founded in 1977 in Seattle, Washington, and works in over 70 countries. PATH has 1200 staff members working from offices in 44 cities within 22 countries. The Viet Nam office is located in Hanoi.

PATH has been working in Viet Nam since 1980 and has expanded its operations from contraceptive technologies to immunisation, maternal and child health, health technologies and more recently research into emerging and infectious diseases as outlined below.

Vaccines and Immunisation

PATH has been working in Viet Nam collaboratively with the National Expanded Program on Immunization (NEPI) since 1997 with the aim of increasing 'the quality, safety and efficiency of Viet Nam's routine immunisation services'. Work towards this aim has resulted in capacity improvement for '3,396 provincial, district and commune health staff' and '3,520 village health workers'. This capacity building has focused on the management and delivery of vaccines to children in remote and rural areas and on supply chain logistics. This has been facilitated through internal partnerships with the National Institute of Hygiene and Epidemiology. Future projects in this space include preparation for a roll-out of the human papillomavirus vaccine and improving the delivery of hepatitis B vaccines to newborn babies.

Reproductive, Maternal and Child Health
As mentioned above, initial work by PATH focused on the provision of condoms and was facilitated through the establishment of a condom manufacturing facility in Ho Chi Minh City. The main driver for this is evidence suggesting that Viet Nam had one of the highest abortion rates, primarily in young, unmarried women. PATH provides contraceptive counselling and products and is also engaged in family planning, ensuring access to safe abortion services where required and postabortion support.

Women are one of two key focus groups, and PATH is working on methods for 'strengthening prevention of cervical cancer' through screening, vaccines and treatment. They are also working with health authorities to develop national guidelines for cervical cancer management.

Women are also the target for midwife capacity building in the management of post-childbirth bleeding which is the leading cause of pregnancy-related deaths in Viet Nam. One project to address this issue resulted in the development of prefilled injection devices for the administration of oxycontin. This solution was created after nurses reported the main barrier to provision of this important bleeding control medication was difficulty in withdrawing the medication from the standard supply ampoules.

The second focus group is children, and PATH's attention has been on preventing the deaths of young children from diarrhoea-related conditions. Diarrhoea is the second cause of death in children in Viet Nam. PATH is again working with government bodies to develop national guidelines on disease control and prevention and is also engaging pharmacists to provide accurate treatment and prevention information and appropriate referral pathways where needed.

Health Technologies
An overarching component of the work done by PATH in Viet Nam is improving access to 'appropriate and affordable health technologies'. This work has focused on:

- Facilitating the safe disposal of medical waste through the use of needle removers and sharps waste disposal protocols.
- Supply chain management for cold chain vaccines. Prior to the implementation of new solar technologies for vaccine supply to communes, only 45 % of babies received a vaccine within the standard 72 h window. After implementation, this rate increased to 83 % within 24 h.

For the future, PATH is testing a battery-powered solution to improve the longevity of current battery-driven solutions and to extend the effectiveness of current solar-powered options. These initiatives not only improve access to the vaccines but also lower the cost of supply which is not inconsequential for refrigerated transport.

Emerging and Epidemic Diseases
Viet Nam is tenth on the WHO's list of 22 countries most impacted by epidemic diseases. PATH's work in this is focused on AIDS, malaria, tuberculosis (TB) and influenza in particular. The work is primarily concerned with:

- Capacity strengthening for pharmacies and clinics in provinces through training staff and clinicians in accurate identification of TB symptoms and understanding referral pathways. This is closely linked with similar work on HIV/AIDS transmission prevention and management. Pharmacies are often the first and only port of call for a Vietnamese who is sick, and this presents a critical point for health education programmes to be embedded.
- Developing a clinical evaluation capacity for the sustainable development, manufacture and evaluation of vaccines in Viet Nam.

6.2 Past Research Objectives and Outcomes

There have been two primary areas of focus for research: professional practice research to facilitate knowledge and skill capacity improvement as part of ongoing professional development and academic research to provide evidence for change through testing new procedures, tools, technologies, treatments or medications.

Research activity is growing in Vietnamese education institutions, but there is still a need for support from international research groups. The primary constraint has been in respect to dissemination of findings as English language capabilities are often not sufficiently strong to secure publications especially in journals outside of Viet Nam. This issue is often solved through engaging in internationally funded research projects. Whilst teaching is almost exclusively done by Vietnamese doctors, several medical schools have international collaboration agreements either for research or specialist training to improve service delivery. This international support is primarily from the USA, Australia (as discussed previously) and Europe with Belgium, Sweden and the Netherlands listed frequently. Most European international collaborations are either focused on visiting specialists conducting trainings and workshops, providing scholarships for students to study abroad or conducting funded research projects [7–9]. The Netherlands conducted a project with eight universities between 2003 and 2009 to strengthen medical skills training across Viet Nam and provided a 900 million VND (approx. 43,000 USD) investment in machines and technology to support medical training and research. A larger project was initiated around e-learning, but given the intended focus on implementing international models of education, this will not continue, and there are three local funding proposals being developed to develop contextualised e-learning infrastructure and capacity. The USA has conducted a range of education projects including strengthening capacity in family medicine which sees only around 120 graduates a year from local universities [10].

International collaboration is seen as critical to improving standards, and ensuring best practice is at least understood, even if not consistently or continuously applied. Collaborative initiatives are often focused on professional development after graduation, and this is particularly important as whilst medical school training is good the body of knowledge continues to evolve (as does the Vietnamese health need landscape as noted previously), but there is little evidence of continued professional development opportunities beyond graduation. Skills development in research is an area that is likely to become a focus for implementation and will provide sustained benefit to Viet Nam; however, there is some reluctance to apply international models of medical training and practice. Any international input to this must be cognisant of the local context and be guided by local academic professionals. When tools, infrastructure and techniques have been the focus of research or knowledge sharing, then the Vietnamese counterparts can then choose how to apply those skills or that knowledge, and this is an important cultural consideration. As with many other areas of operation, research occurs in a very complex landscape, and cultural considerations are paramount for sustained success.

6.3 Current and Future Research Foci

Reducing communicable diseases and strengthening capacity are constantly mentioned as critical areas of need if Vietnamese healthcare is to improve and meet any definition of best practice.

Impactful and sustainable research must begin with developing a clear understanding of the gaps and strategic directions of the country or field of focus. The Vietnamese health landscape, although complex, has been well documented through the 5-year health plan, the GHS and Millennium goals for Viet Nam. The focus areas for current and ongoing research can therefore be summarised.

Controlling pathogens and infectious diseases by providing education and diagnostic tools for early detection remain an area of critical need. HIV/AIDS, MDR TB, dengue and malaria still pose challenges to the public health system, and highly pathogenic virus outbreaks such as avian influenza (H5N1) continue to cause human causalities every year in Viet Nam [11]. Whilst many projects and millions of dollars are being directed at this area, it is still not under control, and continued efforts are required to overcome the current burden of these conditions. This will require:

- A co-ordinated multifaceted approach including public health promotion and prevention campaigns, capacity building in medical professionals, reviews of medical programme content in universities and local infrastructure development including diagnostic testing laboratories and pharmaceutical manufacturing capacity to improve supply chain logistics and availability across the country and lower costs.
- Increased health management capability through a focus on training for senior decision-makers, implementing train-the-trainer initiatives and integrating health management training and skills development into postgraduate programmes, continuing medical education and professional development.
- Reviewed and revised university medical programmes to enable emerging public health issues to be covered and enable new graduates to be better prepared to manage population health in both urban and rural areas and provision of career guidance and incentives to encourage new graduates to build their skills in rural and remote health and in auxiliary health services and support.

- Health literacy improvement across the population through information provision and accessibility for all members of the population should also be implemented. This will encourage appropriate early presentation for diagnosis and treatment and help to reduce the non-communicable disease burden.

Most research has focused on treatment provision and professional capacity building; however, proactive solutions are not sustainable, especially in a country where many lifestyle conditions are only emerging and could be controlled before they reach epidemic proportions.

The GHI Story [12]

The Global Health Initiative (GHI) strategy is a US Government (USG) initiative to support the Government of Viet Nam (GVN) to advance the national healthcare system and provide increased equity, efficiency, affordability and quality for the whole population. The GHI is a collaborative initiative between the President's Emergency Plan for AIDS Relief (PEPFAR), USG-supported Influenza and Emerging Pandemic Threats (EPT) supported by NIH and the Navy Medical Research Unit (NAMRU) and is facilitated and funded by the USG.

GHI priorities have been identified to address some of the most critical areas of need in Viet Nam and aim to develop a more resilient, comprehensive and integrated national health delivery system that is more able to respond to changes in the Vietnamese health landscape. This initiative will integrate the following key activities [12]:

- Develop a national accreditation and quality assurance programme for clinical practice
- Provide continuing medical education opportunities
- Improve access to health services and treatments
- Improve capacity for advanced medical research
- Greater integration of information technology
- Facilitate a more co-ordinated health network across the national, provincial, district and commune level which integrates and provides equity for both the civilian and military sectors
- Support development, implementation and compliance with laws and ministerial directives and circulars
- 'Support research and innovation to address pandemic disease threats and to contribute to the greater knowledge base' to facilitate a strengthening of the national detection and response capacity
- Financially and technically assist with developing improved laboratory capacity, NTD and other zoonotic disease research, virus characterisation, vaccine development capacity and extending disease surveillance and detection to districts and communes

The GHI priorities align with many of Viet Nam's long-term health and development goals as documented in:

- The 5-Year Plan for the Health Sector (2011–2015)

- The National Strategy on Protection, Care and Improvement of the People's Health (2011–2020)
- The 5-Year Socio-Economic Development Plan (2011–2015)

Nearly 80 % of all USG assistance to Viet Nam is directed towards the health sector with support for HIV/AIDS, through PEPFAR, accounting for 90 % of funding. Results to date:

- Antiretroviral therapy has been provided to 28,741 HIV-infected adults and children.
- 355,124 pregnant women have been tested for HIV, and 1238 of those women have been provided with antiretroviral therapy to prevent transmission of HIV to the unborn child.
- HIV counselling and testing have been provided for 42,330 TB patients, and treatment was given to 897 HIV-infected patients newly diagnosed with TB.
- Medication-assisted therapy is provided for 5397 drug users.
- Rural prevention outreach services for 53,043 people at risk for HIV.
- Support to gain ISO accreditation for nine key HIV and TB laboratories.
- Initial accreditation management training for 12 laboratories and follow-up training for 16 laboratories.
- Installation of laboratory information systems in 20 hospital and HIV testing laboratories.
- In-service training for 10,922 healthcare workers to build capacity.
- Improved quality of HIV services.
- Launched and expanded the national quality improvement programme in 68 adult outpatient clinics.
- Developed and updated national policies and testing guidelines for HIV, CD4, viral load testing and training packages.

The measured improvements in HIV and TB management and outcomes in Viet Nam can be directly attributed to the GHI and the sustained, focused activities that have been strategically aligned with the goals of the Vietnamese Government.

The Australia Story

Australia has made a significant investment into research in Viet Nam both financially and through academic and clinical human resources and infrastructure. This is not surprising given that it is the closest western country to Viet Nam and has many Vietnamese students, migrants and products integrated into its suburbs and food culture. Unlike many other countries, Australia has provided capacity building and health services across the whole spectrum of medicine and health including auxiliary services such as ophthalmology, dentistry and physiotherapy. Australia is also the only country to have a sole provider university campus in Viet Nam although they are focused on business and commerce and unfortunately do not offer any health-related programmes.

The following is a representative selection of Australian health projects [13] (Table 6.4).

Table 6.4 Australian-funded projects

Provider	Project	Funding
Centre of Research Excellence on tuberculosis/National Health and Medical Research Council	Building of a Centre of Research Excellence (CRE) on tuberculosis. The research team has members from Australia, Viet Nam, Indonesia and China. It funds PhD and postdoctoral students and organises conferences and capacity building. Senior Vietnamese researchers are core to the team	The Centre is funded by the NHMRC for $3 million over 5 years starting from 2012
Woolcock Institute of Medical Research	Several projects aiming to reduce the prevalence of TB through population screening and genetic testing in several provinces. Australian and Vietnamese medical professionals are included on the local team	$3.4 m for 5 years from 2013. $1.2m over 5 years from 2010
AusAID-UNICEF Partnership on Disability	The project aims to enhance education and child protection systems to be responsive and inclusive of children with disability. Partnerships with the Ministry of Education and Training; Ministry of Health; Ministry of Labour, Invalids and Social Affairs; the World Bank; East Meets West Foundation; Save the Children; Vietnam Veterans of America Foundation; Vietnam Assistance for the Handicapped	106,997.65 AUD, 110,420.50 USD from 2011 to 2013
Queensland University of Technology	Collaborative project with local, national and international partners to improve community health through high-quality collaborative research that advances action in communities and improves university-based training and continuing professional education. Support for PhD study in community and public health	Vietnamese Government study scholarships based in Central Viet Nam. 500,000 USD grant from Atlantic Philanthropies, 200,000 AUD cash contribution from the QUT Vice Chancellor's Strategic Initiative Fund and 300,000 AUD in-kind expenses from provincial health departments and QUT. Duration: 2011–2014
AusAID	Programme to improve the health and living conditions of rural poor by providing clean water and sanitation and by promoting safe hygiene practices. Australia is one of three donors providing targeted budget support and technical assistance	65 million AUD year duration: 2012–2015
Hoc Mai, the Australia Vietnam Medical Foundation, and Sydney Medical School, University of Sydney	Project to establish a research collaboration with Hung Vuong Hospital in HCM City. Collaboratively design and implement a cohort study to investigate the prevalence and outcomes of gestational diabetes in Viet Nam. Vietnamese and Australian project team	IPDF grant total $35,000; Prime Minister's Australia Asia Endeavour Award 2010 $10,000; Hoc Mai Foundation 2010 $4000

(continued)

Table 6.4 (continued)

Provider	Project	Funding
Hoc Mai, the Australia Vietnam Medical Foundation	Several clinical, specialist, education and training programmes and funded overseas placements to provide talented Hanoi Medical University graduates with increased medical English and clinical skills to enable them to become future academic and health leaders	120,000 AUD per year to support 150 students per year
University of Sydney with Hanoi Medical University and Pham Ngoc Thach University	Project to develop undergraduate, university courses in speech pathology in Viet Nam. Seven fellows from Vietnamese universities sponsored to visit the University of Sydney to work with speech therapy academics and learn about speech therapy curriculum development, assessment and standards of practice, so programmes can be developed for Viet Nam	AusAID award 68,653.00 AUD for 2 years from September 2013
Operation Smile Australia	Craniofacial medical missions assist specialist medical professionals to travel to Viet Nam and provide full consultation and treatment for 10–20 children and young adults and surgery for 5–10 patients each year	Annual fundraising, donations and pro bono work of specialists
AusAID	Provision of harm reduction services and information to more than 34,500 people who inject drugs in the Greater Mekong Subregion and distribution of over 2.4 million condoms, 1.3 million sterile water vials and 6.3 million needles and syringes at targeted sites	13 million AUD to 2013
AusAID	Foster strategic partnerships and linkages between Australia and the Asia-Pacific region to increase the capacity of partners to contribute to effective HIV responses. The programme does this by funding projects that link Australian organisations with regional counterparts	59 million AUD over 9 years from 2010
University of Melbourne Centre for International Mental Health	Strengthen leadership for mental health system development in Viet Nam. The activity will support training of 25 people over 4 years	University of Melbourne and AusAID 485,254 AUD since 2010

6.4 Success Factors for Applied Research

There are hundreds of millions of dollars invested into health research and clinical projects in Viet Nam each year; however, too often the results are minimal or short-lived with little sustained benefit for Viet Nam and its people. There is a need for all researchers or commercial entities to understand the landscape that they are hoping to move into. Nowhere is this more true than in Viet Nam where doing things in the right way is vitally important culturally, commercially and politically. The people are well educated and open to positive change but do not want to be 'taken over' or dictated to by external parties. Whilst Viet Nam may seem to present an impenetrable environment given the lack of (and unreliability of) information in the public domain, the political system, complex language and reports of commercial operational difficulties, however the general population and ministry stakeholders are incredibly accommodating if they can see that they can participate in initiatives and there are benefits to be gained for their country. If approached in an intelligent and informed manner, Viet Nam can be a very positive and accommodating place to work and do research.

The stories on PATH, the GHI and other initiatives and groups working in Viet Nam together with newspaper articles have provided a diverse picture of health research and capacity improvement projects conducted by government, academic, NGO and international entities within the Vietnamese health context. Whilst these stories have provided different perspectives, it is possible to identify a number of common characteristics or success factors in all of the initiatives or operational strategies of those who achieve their aims. If understood and incorporated, these characteristics can provide a high level of confidence that a successful outcome can be achieved. These characteristics are:

- Having the ability to accommodate a growing web of interlaced projects often developing as subprojects out of each other to facilitate a holistic, integrated and sustainable solution
- Being funded by a range of external donors both governmental and non-governmental
- Engaging in a long-term investment with a defined focus and measurable, quantified outcomes that align with national priority areas
- Taking a collaborative approach and using a range of local and international expertise to drive progress based on world best practice whilst providing culturally appropriate solutions
- Embedding capacity building for local communities to ensure sustainability of outcomes
- Building support from government and local enterprise prior to implementation

These characteristics are seen as critical success factors in high-performing research and practical healthcare projects in Viet Nam. Ignoring any one of these will present a barrier to meeting objectives, result in reluctance to engage locally or see outcomes quickly become diluted and unsustainable.

References

1. United Nations (2011) Viet Nam annual report 2011. www.un.org.vn. Accessed 10 Oct 2014
2. USAID (n.d.) Barriers to access and use of public TB diagnostic services in Vietnam
3. PATH (2000) Improving health in Vietnam celebrating 30 years of partnership. www.path.org/publications/files/CP_vietnam_bro.pdf. Accessed 18 Dec 2014

4. PATH (2011) Controlling diarrheal disease in Vietnam. www.path.org/publications/files/CP_vietnam_dd_fs.pdf. Accessed 18 Dec 2014
5. PATH (2012) Vietnam: demonstrating innovative health supply chain solutions. www.path.org/publications/files/TS_opt_vietnam.pdf. Accessed 18 Dec 2014
6. PATH (n.d.) Leveraging the capacity of pharmacies to improve health outcomes in Vietnam. www.path.org/publications/files/VN_pharm_fs.pdf. Accessed 18 Dec 2014
7. portal.ctump.edu.vn/en/index.php?option=com_content&view=category&layout=blog&id=215&Itemid=243. Accessed 12 Oct 2014
8. www.bu.edu/ghc/where-we-work/viet-nam-projects/vietnam-family/. Accessed 13 Oct 2014
9. www.pnt.edu.vn/home/H%E1%BB%A3p-tac-qu%E1%BB%91c-t%E1%BA%BF/thong-tin-chung.html. Accessed 9 Oct 2014
10. Tran H, Pretorius R (2008) Vietnamese [sic] medical education and development of family medicine in Vietnam. State University of New York at Buffalo School of Medicine and Biomedical Sciences. VMGUS Publication No 052009, New York
11. U.S. Government Global Health Initiative Strategy (2011) Vietnam V5.0. Aug 2011
12. Centres for Disease Control and Prevention (2014) www.cdc.gov/globalhealth/countries/vietnam/. Accessed 12 Dec 2014
13. Hoc Mai Foundation and University of Sydney (2013) Together for health. An overview of Australia's involvement within Vietnam's health care sector. University of Sydney, p 38

Chapter 7
The Top Ten Health Issues in Viet Nam

Whilst addressing defined areas of focus for the Government of Viet Nam is a reasonable strategy, it is important to acknowledge that the strategies and priority areas in any 5-year plan (or other government document) may become obsolete and new ones may emerge, and hence these documents may not accurately reflect the current state of healthcare so should not be considered the single source of truth. Relying solely on these documents to gain an understanding of the healthcare context in Viet Nam may not therefore be the most appropriate methodology, especially if there is a significant and long-term investment of any kind involved. Whilst understanding what the current areas of research and commercial development focus and gaps are important, there should also be consideration of what is having the greatest impact. In a population of 90 million people, any health concern with a high prevalence, cost or increasing incidence is worthy of attention, even if not currently a government or other priority. Unfortunately Viet Nam is yet to reach a high level of maturity in terms of data collection and management and given its history, there are few complete data sets and little comprehensive longitudinal data especially prior to 2000. It is therefore difficult to develop an accurate picture of the true situation or measure the effect of programmes and policies. This problem is exacerbated by many of the cultural issues and barriers to healthcare access discussed earlier. When looking at data for the cause of death, we must be mindful that several tens of thousands of people would die in a year with no true account or recording of the cause and we should not rely on actual raw numbers but instead use percentage of deaths attributed to a cause or within a location as an indicator to base decisions on.

7.1 Health Issues Ranking

This section will provide an overview of the top 10 health issues in Viet Nam and will provide an insight into the ranking trends over the duration of the past two 5-year plans (Tables 7.1 and 7.2).

A.G. Shillabeer, *The Health of Vietnam*, DOI 10.1007/978-981-287-709-3_7

Table 7.1 The leading causes of death in Viet Nam in 2003 [1]

Top 10 leading causes of mortality 2003	Number recorded	Rate per 100,000 population
1. Intracranial injuries	2327	2.88
2. Pneumonia	1374	1.70
3. HIV	1260	1.56
4. Transport accident	1230	1.52
5. Intracerebral haemorrhage	1181	1.46
6. Stroke, not specified as haemorrhage	922	1.14
7. Heart failure	779	0.96
8. Acute myocardial infarct	733	0.91
9. Respiratory tuberculosis	723	0.89
10. Septicaemia	638	0.79

Table 7.2 The leading causes of death in Viet Nam in 2010 [2]

Top 10 causes of mortality in 2010 (69% of all deaths recorded)	Number recorded	% deaths VN/world
1. Cancer	133,425	25/14.7
2. Stroke	106,740	20/11.9
3. Ischaemic heart disease	32,022	6/13.2
4. Chronic obstructive pulmonary disease	21,348	4/5.6
5. Lower respiratory infections	21,348	4/5.5
6. Tuberculosis	21,348	4/1.7
7. Road injuries	21,348	4/2.3
8. Cirrhosis	16,011	3/1.8
9. HIV	16,011	3/2.8
10. Diabetes	16,011	3/2.7

It quickly becomes obvious that there has been a significant shift in the primary cause of deaths in Viet Nam from injuries, HIV and pneumonia to more western-pattern health issues such as cancer, stroke and heart disease. Of interest is the apparent emergence of TB which may explain the focus on TB in a number of large research projects. This 'emergence' should be viewed as a result of improved data capture rather than suggestive that there was a low level of TB prior to 2000. The significant drop in HIV rates could also be attributed to focused research projects and more accurate diagnosis and recording but again this is not conclusive as data prior to the commencement of the projects was likely not reliable. New helmet laws have come into effect (although are often ignored!) between these data collection dates, but again data collection in general on traffic accidents, injuries and deaths has improved and hence we should take care when attributing patterns or causality to any suggested trends. Even if the data is not accurate, we can gain some insight into the logic behind the government strategic focus at a point in time and better understand why some decisions were made and what the determinants were for identification of national priorities.

To generalise, road trauma, heart disease, respiratory illness, cancer, stroke, haemorrhage and HIV continue to be major health issues for the Vietnamese health sector and will continue to be so into the next 5-year plan. New trends that are emerging and will continue to grow include nutritional issues, especially obesity, lifestyle issues including stress and cardiovascular disease and conditions associated with aging including dementia and falls. There are few focusing on these issues but until they become listed in the health impact rankings by organisations such as the WHO, they are unlikely to become a government priority and therefore world target for research attention. As always, prevention should be the aim before expensive, resource-intensive and time-consuming cures are required. In this respect, knowledge on emerging health issues is potentially more powerful than knowledge of existing and uncontrolled issues that already feature in major commercial and research initiatives.

If the most recent top 10 list is compared to specialisations being taught in universities and priorities in the current 5-year plan by the ministry, it is possible to see that a review is needed to meet the emerging demand and change in trends which is already making an impact. Given that a new 5-year plan will not be implemented for another 2 years and any medical programme changes will not be reflected in practice for at least 6 years, it may already be too late to stem the tide and minimise the potential damage.

The table below suggests that there needs to be an alignment between the current and future health needs of Viet Nam, the education for medical professionals and government support for programmes to ensure that there is the required capacity and infrastructure to meet what will be a growing and potentially insurmountable demand if appropriate measures are not taken (Table 7.3).

Table 7.3 Comparison between top health issues, education to provide capacity and government strategic focus

Top 10 causes of mortality in 2010	# of universities with specialisation	Government priority
1. Cancer	3	Yes
2. Stroke	0	No
3. Ischaemic heart disease	0	No
4. Chronic obstructive pulmonary disease	0	Yes
5. Lower respiratory infections	0	No
6. Tuberculosis	3	Yes
7. Road injuries	0	No
8. Cirrhosis	0	No
9. HIV	3	Yes
10. Diabetes	1	Yes

7.2 The Social and Financial Burden

There are a wide range of social impacts resulting from the healthcare framework in Viet Nam. As mentioned earlier the social impact of the loss of an income for a household is significant and when that person needs to be cared for by family, the burden may be felt by an entire community. The cost of treatment and relocation expenses can often leave a family in financial crisis and so primary healthcare is often avoided. In the case of communicable diseases, this can mean rapid transmission and the lives or livelihoods of many being put at risk.

Research has shown that for some diseases, there are significant savings that could be made for patients and the healthcare system as a whole. For example, in the case of cardiovascular disease, there are potential savings for the healthcare budget of between 1.28 and 10.16 million (approximately $60–550) in terms of Vietnamese Dong (VND) per DALY saved by implementing a mass media campaign with messages to reduce salt intake and cholesterol [3]. From a patient perspective, other research comparing the costs for peritoneal dialysis (PD) and haemodialysis (HD) evidenced that the cost to patients for PD at home was about half than that for the default HD at hospital without impacting on efficacy [4, 5]. The total savings across the participant group were approximately USD$2400 per month and this represented a small proportion of the total population undergoing dialysis. The added benefit of PD is that the patient can receive treatment at home thus providing an opportunity to reduce the need for a hospital bed and increase the opportunity for the patient to be cared for by family in their own home.

Whilst the financial implications and possible savings are important for those suffering from disease at any point in time, the cost in terms of lives lost is more socially significant and can have a greater impact on families and communities. The number of excess lives lost in Viet Nam can be calculated by comparing the mortality rates in Viet Nam against the world as listed in the rankings above. From this we can predict the number of deaths that would be expected in Viet Nam if the same average world death rates for the top 10 causes of mortality were applied.

The results of this comparison are shown in Table 7.4 and show the number of excessive or lower deaths occurring in Viet Nam.

Table 7.4 provides both good and bad news for sufferers of the listed conditions. The predictions evidence that approximately 133,100 people die in Viet Nam that would not have been lost if average world survival rates were met. More positively 53,200 people survived that would not have done so if world death rates were met; however, there is still a 79,900 deficit which in some countries represents a whole town lost needlessly. This number represents approximately 15 % of all deaths in Viet Nam.

These numbers define the real areas for future attention by government and research institutes around the world. Any extra life lost should be viewed as a tragedy and the numbers in the table should be considered to be lower than actual numbers due to data quality and diagnosis avoidance issues discussed previously. The actual deficit is therefore likely to be much higher.

Table 7.4 Comparison of deaths due to top 10 mortality causes

Top 10 causes of mortality in 2010	# recorded	% deaths VN/world	Approx # of deaths in Viet Nam at world %	Approx difference in # of deaths
Cancer	133,425	25/14.7	80,000	+53,500
Stroke	106,740	20/11.9	64,000	+43,000
Ischaemic heart disease	32,022	6/13.2	70,000	−38,000
COPD	21,348	4/5.6	29,000	−7600
Lower respiratory infections	21,348	4/5.5	29,000	−7600
Tuberculosis	21,348	4/1.7	8500	+12,800
Road injuries	21,348	4/2.3	11,000	+10,300
Cirrhosis	16,011	3/1.8	9000	+7000
HIV	16,011	3/2.8	13,000	+3000
Diabetes	16,011	3/2.7	12,500	+3500

References

1. World Health Organisation (2005) Viet Nam: health profile. www.who.int/gho/countries/vnm.pdf. Accessed 14 Aug 2014
2. Centres for Disease Control and Prevention (2014) www.cdc.gov/globalhealth/countries/vietnam/. Accessed 12 Dec 2014
3. Duc HA, Chisholm D (2011) Cost-effectiveness analysis of interventions to prevent cardiovascular disease in Vietnam. Health Policy Plan 26:210–222. doi:10.1093/heapol/czq045, Oxford University Press
4. Vietnamese Family Health. Health beliefs and healing practices. www.vietfamilyhealth.org/culture/beliefs.html. Accessed 12 Jan 2015
5. Pham KYH, Phan BV (2013) Comparison of peritoneal dialysis and hemodialysis at People's Hospital 115 – Ho Chi Minh City – a cost utility analysis. http://chsr.org.vn/en/wp-content/uploads/2013/11/So-s%C3%A1nh-l%E1%BB%8Dc-m%C3%A0ng-b%E1%BB%A5ng-v%C3%A0-l%E1%BB%8Dc-th%E1%BA%ADn-English1.pdf. Accessed 9 Jan 2015

Chapter 8
The Future

8.1 Opportunities and Barriers for Improvement in Healthcare Outcomes

The top health issues for Viet Nam both currently and for the future have been discussed in previous sections. These present opportunities to expand current research projects and commercial opportunities and to develop new industries and research foci for the future. There has been significant progress in Vietnamese healthcare outcomes over the past 15 years in particular, but there are still many opportunities for new players to enter the market and for existing players to expand operations.

Key areas requiring focus for the future are in practice capacity building (infrastructure and human resources) especially in rural areas, health technology leverage and development of national health information systems and data management standards, preventative health programmes and health literacy improvement, health management and policy development capability building, reduction of the service provision and access disparity across Viet Nam, implementation of an independent medical education quality assessment and national accreditation process, regulation for compulsory national medical practitioner licencing, development of recognised programmes of continuing medical education and development of analytical capacity to facilitate identification of emerging trends in healthcare to enable proactive rather than reactive solutions.

The opportunity for improvement in Vietnamese health systems and processes is presented in all areas of healthcare, but there are a number of barriers to be overcome to both facilitate entry and ensure sustainability. The main barriers within Viet Nam include cultural traditions; the lack of capacity and time to build that capacity; the need to build trust within the industry and the government for programmes to be supported, facilitated and approved for implementation; the lack of clinical and infrastructure service and support in rural areas and hence 70 % of the population; a lack of affordability for the majority of the population exacerbated by 'secret payments' leading to under-reporting of demand and therefore a lack of planning for

A.G. Shillabeer, *The Health of Vietnam*, DOI 10.1007/978-981-287-709-3_8

increased service provision; poor technical infrastructure support and training after delivery and installation leading to machinery breakdown, misuse or non-use, urban migration and demand beyond the ability of the health sector to supply in major cities; and a lack of funding to initiate or sustain initiatives.

The commercial healthcare focus is primarily targeted towards building private hospitals and clinics. The interest in expanding the private healthcare sector is based on the common knowledge that demand outstrips supply of hospital beds and medical practitioners; however, there are concerns regarding the appropriateness of the solution to solve the problem. Deeper analysis, as discussed in earlier sections, reveals that there is a huge gap between the demands in the public and private sector, and it is the public sector that is at breaking point, whilst the private sector is significantly underutilised.

Expanding the private sector will not alleviate the overcrowding and access disparity problems that are currently crippling the industry. Developing the private sector may open up health tourism opportunities for Viet Nam, but the question then is regarding the utilisation of the resultant revenue streams whether there is the potential to direct that towards improving access to healthcare for all Vietnamese or whether it will stay with the private companies and their directors.

In the News [1]

With Viet Nam's public hospitals stretched beyond their limits and private healthcare a fledgling sector, there are billions to be made courting deep-pocketed Vietnamese for medical treatment overseas.

It's a tidy niche that one former Vietnamese medical student carved out for herself. She made \$3200 a month – 20 times the average income of her peers – working the phones to earn hospitals in nearby Singapore a slice of the \$2 billion that Viet Nam haemorrhaged on overseas healthcare last year.

With that flight of overseas cash equivalent to 60 % of state health spending, private operators both foreign and domestic are smelling opportunity in keeping that in Viet Nam. Local conglomerate Vingroup is planning huge hospital expansion from next year.

Some 40,000 Vietnamese a year won't take their chances with the snaking queues, chronic bed shortages and overworked doctors at home. Whilst Viet Nam's medical spending as a percentage of the economy is the highest in Southeast Asia, it hasn't kept up with the population's demand for quality and timely medical care.

'It's a matter of trust. They don't feel safe in Vietnam', said the former student, who spoke on condition of anonymity. 'Viet Nam only has a few private hospitals, a drop in the ocean, and people with money prefer to go to a pricier place with certified and better doctors'.

Viet Nam has a 90 million population, and its middle class is expected to grow five times bigger in size by 2020, owing to annual economic growth of over 5 % since 1999.

According to a 2014 report by property consultant Frank Knight, the communist country also has the world's fastest-growing number of super rich, with Vietnamese holding net assets of \$30 million projected to swell to 293 from 110 in a decade.

But the wealthy have limited options. Private facilities are used by just 7 % of Vietnamese, and that adds strain to packed public hospitals where waiting time averages 4–7 h and bed occupancy can be 170 %, according to the Health Ministry.

In 2012, Viet Nam's health spending was the highest in the region as a percentage of gross domestic product, the latest data from the World Health Organisation shows. But at $102 per capita, that's less than half of Thailand's, a quarter of Malaysia and about 4 % of Singapore.

Overstretched, Overrun

'Capacity in cancer, cardiac, orthopaedic and paediatrics is severely lacking, and a specialist working in a city can receive as many as 100 patients per day', the ministry says.

'Facilities are a big problem', said Deepak Arora, an Indian expatriate who was treated at a private hospital in Hanoi, but went to India for a second opinion. 'Local hospitals are very good, but they're overpacked'.

The state put $3.4 billion into over 1,000 public hospitals last year, but the number of patients outstrips capacity.

The private health sector can't shoulder the growing burden either, and a bad debt problem among local banks has tightened commercial lending. The number of private hospitals more than quadrupled to 170 over the past decade, but about half are 'dying or dead', chairman of the Association of Vietnamese Private Hospitals, Nguyen Van De, said in March.

The government is welcoming international firms to fill that void, promising no restrictions on qualified foreign doctors to practise in Viet Nam, deputy health minister Nguyen Thanh Long said last month.

Among interested firms are Thailand's Bumrungrad Hospital PCL and Indonesian conglomerate Lippo Group, which wants to build 15 hospitals in Viet Nam. Malaysia's IHH healthcare Bhd is scouting sites in Hanoi.

'We are looking at Viet Nam too since there is good potential', said Engku Mashuri Engku Hussein of Malaysia's KPJ healthcare Bhd, which wants to offer consultancy and management services. 'If we take 10 percent of the population can afford private health care, that means 9 million people'.

Stemming the Flow

Leading the domestic healthcare drive is Viet Nam's fourth biggest listed firm, Vingroup, whose billionaire founder Pham Nhat Vuong built his empire from instant noodles in Ukraine to malls, private schools, condominiums, e-commerce and more.

It will increase its private hospitals, known as Vinmec, to ten from one within 5 years and will complete construction of a medical university in 2015. Vinmec's early focus will be cancer, cardiac, paediatrics and stem cells.

'Our group sees this is a potential market as the medical need from Vietnamese is increasing', Nguyen Thanh Liem, the head of Vinmec in Hanoi, told Reuters. 'Why do we need to go abroad?'

Vinmec wants certification from Joint Commission International, which rates medical safety standards and has accredited 37 Thai, 13 Malaysian and 21 Singaporean hospitals, but only one so far in Viet Nam.

Vinmec is following the lead of Thailand, Singapore and Malaysia in targeting medical tourists with hospitals in travel hotspots Ho Chi Minh City, Phu Quoc, Nha Trang and Ha Long.

Though three quarters of Vietnamese are entitled to state social insurance, the health ministry says 'about half those covered pay out of pocket for treatment and are willing to pay for better care'.

8.2 Road Map for an Improved Healthcare Environment in Viet Nam

Viet Nam presents a vibrant and broad landscape in which to implement change and directly impact the quality of millions of human lives. It is one of the few places left where even small groups of researchers or small- to medium-sized commercial entities can have a real measured impact on healthcare of an entire country. However, there are foundations to be built and strong bridges to be constructed; this is not a 'plug and play' environment where solutions can simply be shipped in and implemented directly. The next major milestone for Vietnamese healthcare is 2020. This is when the Ministry of Health and other key stakeholders hope to implement their new healthcare vision for Viet Nam. This vision essentially encapsulates all of the work done to date and aims to have Viet Nam recognised both locally and internationally as a provider of quality healthcare education, services, research, treatment, policy and above all innovative solutions to improve the quality of life for all Vietnamese. In early 2015 the question is: Will Viet Nam be ready for this healthcare revolution? The answer? Maybe, maybe not! There is much work being done by many people with hundreds of millions of dollars being invested but little big-picture planning or programme management to ensure that all of the pieces will be in place. Experience in Viet Nam suggests that there is either too fine a focus on the detail, when a high-level picture needs to be developed to understand the connectivity and broad impact of decisions, or decision-makers are looking at an abstract view without understanding the detail and hence the intricacies of bringing that view to reality. Both of these issues cause delays, road blocks and rework. There is also insufficient risk management implemented, but that is a whole other book.

There are six pillars upon which a foundation must be built before 2020. These can be broadly categorised as education; clinical standards; management and technology support services; infrastructure strengthening; policy, procedure and legal frameworks; and population culture change. Given these pillars a road map is required to facilitate Viet Nam reaching a state of readiness in each of these areas by 2020. There will need to be immediate progress with international expert input to each pillar and potentially to manage and guide the overall change programme and ensure individual projects to stay on track. Following is a high-level road map with key activities and milestones, which if met, will provide a level of assurance that the intended revitalisation of the Vietnamese healthcare system in line with international standards can be facilitated from 2020. It is noted that some of the activities required for preparation have already been achieved and hence are not listed below.

8.2.1 Education

Medical education quality influences every aspect of the healthcare system in any country. Undergraduate programmes should prepare graduates for entry-level professional practice in general medicine. Graduates should have acquired the minimum competencies including the prerequisites for any relevant licencing, be equipped for lifelong learning and professional development, understand the trends and treatment of the most prevalent diseases and medical issues in the country and be able to pursue any field of specialisation through postgraduate study. Viet Nam does not yet have statements of medical practitioner competencies or national guidelines on required graduate outcomes at any level. There are also no competency requirements for academic staff or any quality assurance or review processes mandated for. Also lacking is the provision of continuing medical education, and professional development opportunities to ensure skills are sustained and developed to meet changing needs. Raising the quality of education raises the quality of graduates and thus improves the provision of healthcare by practitioners in all health fields over time (Table 8.1).

8.2.2 Clinical Standards

When medical education provides the highest possible graduate preparedness, both in terms of skills and personal attributes, the next step is to ensure that practising professionals maintain and develop those skills. Requiring a licence to practice not only provides a level of confidence that minimum competencies are being met, and hence patients and facilities can feel safe in the knowledge that treating professionals are registered and meet approved quality standards. It also provides an opportunity to identify professional development needs and assess the appropriateness of

Table 8.1 Milestones for medical education

Activity	Milestone
Develop medical education programme and provider standards	Mid 2015
Develop and implement independent accreditation for all medical universities and medical programmes	End 2017
Develop and implement primary and secondary school health education programmes	End 2018
Review all higher education medical programmes and revise to ensure relevancy and future proofing	End 2017
Develop and implement e-learning platforms for delivery of nationwide CME and PD	End 2018
Develop research capacity and identify mentors for every medical university	End 2018
Develop and deliver nationwide workshops to ensure all in practice medical professionals meet minimum competencies	End 2018
Identify skills and competency gaps and develop strategy to address needs	End 2016

Table 8.2 Milestones for clinical standards

Activity	Milestone
Develop practice standards and identify minimum professional competencies for each health field	Mid 2016
Develop and implement professional licencing for all medical professionals	End 2018
Develop and implement medical professional quality assurance processes	End 2017
Identify and implement global best practice for the top 10 health issues in Viet Nam	End 2018
Develop and implement medical location quality assurance and minimum standards	End 2018
Develop and implement medical location accreditation process	End 2019

education programmes. Clinical facilities should also undergo assessment and accreditation to ensure all practices, treatments and technologies are safe, appropriate and well managed. Global best practice has been the focus of some research, and evidence suggests that there are opportunities to reduce cost and improve efficacy, quality of life and/or safety for patients. Understanding and implementing global best practice will again provide an assurance that the highest quality healthcare is being provided (Table 8.2).

8.2.3 Management and Technology Support Services

The key issue slowing progress generally in Viet Nam is a lack of management skills and training. This is of particular concern in healthcare where lives are potentially at stake if wrong decisions are made, and where the landscape is in flux, and hence there is a need for significant change management capacity. There are currently no health management training opportunities in Viet Nam and few overseas opportunities promoted. Unfortunately, this lack of appropriate management expertise results in a lack of ability to implement evidence-based practice, monitor standards, identify opportunities and threats and proactively implement measures to manage changing trends and healthcaref needs of defined populations. Most managers are placed into management positions due to longevity or natural gravitation and have never been trained in key management skills such as finance, human and other resource planning and monitoring, quality assurance, project and programme management and procurement (Table 8.3).

Health Infrastructure and technology management which underpins strategy development, resource management and clinical service provision in Viet Nam is also experiencing significant problems as there is no national record of what technology has been procured or is being used, what technologies have been developed/installed locally to manage information or clinical processes, what technical solutions are needed or where the skill gaps are in users to enable appropriate use and management. There is also little knowledge at the management level regarding maintenance and licencing of technology. Often technology is provided through international research grants, but there is no central record, no local training and no service agreements which too often means no sustainable use after a project ends.

Table 8.3 Milestones for management and technology support services

Activity	Milestone
Identify minimum standards for health managers	End 2015
Develop and implement SLAs with all hardware and software providers	End 2015
Develop and implement health management skills training across Viet Nam	End 2017
Provide technical training for all support staff in national infrastructure and management systems	End 2016
Develop and implement a national procurement and resource management IT system	End 2018
Audit all clinical and health management technology and develop a national strategy to manage and standardise	End 2016
Develop and implement a postgraduate health management programme	End 2019

Table 8.4 Milestones for information management strengthening

Activity	Milestone
Develop information management and data security standards	End 2015
Develop national minimum data set for health	End 2016
Develop and implement a national health data system	End 2018
Develop and implement a national electronic patient records system	End 2018
Provide every patient contact point with a data input device	End 2017
Develop and implement information systems and basic security training for at least one person at each patient contact point	End 2017
Develop and implement a national laboratory test records system	End 2018

8.2.4 Information Management Strengthening

Information systems are the foundation of health structures in western and many Asian countries, but in Viet Nam, there has been minimal progress realised. Patients still have to carry hard copies of test requests and results between buildings or providers (and pay if they are lost in transit) and have to resupply all information, history and documentation when visiting a new clinician. There is almost no automation of medical records and no national systems to collect or analyse data (Table 8.4).

Further compounding the issue is that there are very few laws on information and data collection, management and security in general and even fewer laws respected, implemented and appropriated for health. This scenario not only negatively impacts on clinical and management processes but also on compliance when international reporting is required for research funding reporting and audits, etc. when documents cannot be found and there is no record of the assigned responsible party or storage location.

This lack of co-ordinated information management negatively affects management decision-making and planning, financial processing, patient management and general documentation.

Table 8.5 Milestones for policy procedure and legal frameworks

Activity	Milestone
Finalise law on treatment and practice	End 2015
Develop national education and clinical facility accreditation law and policy	End 2016
Develop law and policy on professional licencing and directives to guide CME and PD and competency development and maintenance	End 2017
Develop directive for new pre-tertiary health education curriculum	End 2017
Develop competency in evidence- and trend-based approaches to developing health policy and plans	End 2018
Develop directives on application of global best practice in all aspects of medicine and healthcare	End 2018
Develop policy to guide standardisation of clinical technology and health information systems procurement and management	End 2016

8.2.5 Policy, Procedure and Legal Frameworks

There is no national information system infrastructure, policy, standards, security mechanism, registration, maintenance or training. The implications of this are too many to list, but they impact upon the potential to build and manage any of the other pillars effectively or sustainably. If managers cannot access data and information to apply to planning and operational decisions, clinicians cannot access test results and treatment histories for their patients, systems across the country operate in isolation and do not exhibit connectivity, there are no implemented compliance assessments or penalties for non-compliance and then the system is bound to fail. A failure of the health system can result in anything from mild inconvenience through delays in an administrative process to a catastrophic event through loss of patient records in a database or inability to realise the presence of a potential epidemic (Table 8.5).

Good policy and legal frameworks may not prevent every possible risk from eventuating, but it will provide a good level of confidence that best practice, as understood at a point in time, is being applied and that nothing more could have been done. This is a critical distinction in terms of developing and maintaining international credibility and encouraging the population to develop trust in their own healthcare system and engage appropriately which will influence better outcomes and faster recoveries and improve the overall ranking for Viet Nam.

8.2.6 Population Culture Change

Changing cultural and traditional behaviours and beliefs is a long-term process and requires mentors or champions and an iterative education and community awareness programme that does not ignore or prevent access to traditional health pathways and practices but encourages and informs where there are options and where those options may provide better outcomes. Whilst this pillar is not critical to implementing the

Table 8.6 Milestones for population culture change

Activity	Milestone
Promote services and quality improvements in healthcare structures	End 2016
Ensure equitable access for all and promote understanding of availability	End 2018
Assess and address health literacy gaps to allow self-management of general health and develop a culture of prevention rather than cure	End 2018
Provide equitable access to healthcare services and develop specialist competencies in rural and remote healthcare services	End 2019
Develop trusted community support groups in areas of relevant focus for the location	End 2017

intended changes in healthcare, acceptance is critical to sustain initiatives and maintain viability. If a service is expanded or initiated but no one takes advantage of its availability, then it represents a poor investment, and the resources would be better employed where there is demand and no net gain will be realised in the original community, thus triggering a return to the status quo (Table 8.6).

References

1. Nguyen M (2014) Vietnam preps for medical makeover to recoup lost billions in health care. Tue 14 Oct 2014. www.reuters.com/article/2014/10/14/vietnam-healthcare-idUSL3N0S33FD20141014. Accessed 9 Dec 2014

Chapter 9
Conclusion

Viet Nam is a wonderful country of contradiction, consistency, conflict, culture and a critical need to improve its national health systems. Viet Nam is also a country that has the drive, passion, self-belief and sheer bloody mindedness to never give up on its goals to revolutionise the delivery of healthcare, but it cannot do this alone. Whilst the key building blocks for reform, investment, education, tools and technologies are evidenced, the missing link is the human capacity to mobilise and drive the initiatives to fruition then maintain them. There has been significant support and input from the international community but care must be taken to ensure sustainability by empowering and building the people. Too often research is done (important research that has the potential to change the lives of millions), outcomes are achieved and reported, and many thousands of dollars of equipment are installed, but when the research team leaves or moves to the next project, so does the benefit and new competencies at the grass-roots level. This may be because of insufficient training or up-skilling or because the time has not been taken to develop the deep relationships with appropriate ministries, local universities or other local entities that can provide sustainability. We as scientific researchers are not always good at this softer side of our work, but Viet Nam calls for a different balance, a broader team composition and a more holistic approach. Viet Nam does not have major research organisations to provide the network connectivity, promotion and relationship management function that we in the west take for advantage, but without this our research means nothing and will fade into obscurity. Whilst commercial entities are a little better at networking and building relationships, it can be difficult in a country with a very different language, culture and business operational environment so again, local support, intelligence and connections are necessary for sustained success. Navigating the laws, taxation requirements and implications of ownership models and getting the best deal or right advice are near impossible without trusted local input. The Vietnamese stakeholders also need to better understand how the west works and how they can get the most advantage from what is available in terms of solutions, collaborations, funding and human resources. They must become better at being proactive, understanding how to network with western entities and

A.G. Shillabeer, *The Health of Vietnam*, DOI 10.1007/978-981-287-709-3_9

build confidence in their ability to take and maintain control over projects. Neither local nor international entities can function in isolation and expect success but neither wants to feel controlled or dictated to so care is needed to build the correct frameworks. This book has highlighted the components of those frameworks and suggested a pathway through the maze. Each entity needs to mould an operational model around those components that is unique to meet its own (and Viet Nam's) needs for each project.

This book has identified a number of key areas to be addressed if Vietnamese healthcare is to be recognised as high quality and up to world standard. These areas are:

- A growing need for world class, effective and cost-efficient health services to identify and meet current and future trends in disease patterns, morbidity and mortality regardless of location.
- Health sector management strengthening to support good strategic and operational implementation. Many health facilities are deteriorating, medical equipment is out of date or unused, there are shortages of qualified, and skilled health workers and technicians and reform policies and mechanisms are delayed.
- Health literacy and prevention programmes are needed to keep people out of the healthcare system where possible and to alleviate the problems of overcrowding, long waiting times and emerging lifestyle-predicated public health issues.
- The urban focus and a growing, unregulated private health sector have created gaps in the system especially for the rural poor who are experiencing increasingly inequitable access to health services.
- International investment and collaboration in health have increased but are often fragmented, not sustained and does not sufficiently empower the local population or professionals.
- Education systems need to be of world standard to provide a strong professional practice foundation, and accreditation for both education and clinical facilities is required to provide evidence for future strategy, policy, research, investment and collaboration focus and motivation.

Viet Nam is changing and rapidly. It has new-found wealth and access to goods and services that could only be dreamt of a generation ago but economic development and changing lifestyles are contributing to changing disease patterns with a higher percentage of non-communicable diseases stressing an already overburdened healthcare system. This presents an exciting and challenging environment for global research and commercial enterprises to enter and operate in; however, international entities cannot (and should not try to) bend Viet Nam to the ways of the west but should work as equals with the Vietnamese to develop and implement unique solutions that are sustainable and valuable for the whole population. We can change lives and nations and if our work is appropriate for Viet Nam then it presents opportunities to benefit neighbouring countries also. This is the next global frontier for healthcare mobilisation and innovation but it will need a co-ordinated approach with strong programme, fiscal and resource management at the national level. A combination of the knowledge, experience and funding opportunities of the international community and the dedication, proud traditions and desire to grow human and organisational capacity that is evident in Viet Nam can facilitate truly nation-changing outcomes that could make a difference to over 90 million lives and save tens of thousands each year.

This book has identified the complexities and barriers that exist in the Vietnamese healthcare context but has also highlighted the exciting opportunities that exist. The Vietnamese are an intelligent, hard-working, resilient, future-thinking people that are ready to change and deserve a chance to do so. When the knowledge to facilitate that change and save lives is available, it would be morally negligent not to engage.

Final Word

Healthcare innovation in Viet Nam should be driven by its people not its past. The west can provide a map but we must enable the Vietnamese people to read it so that they may travel to any destination at any time.

Appendix A

Medical programme schedule and course content for all medical undergraduate programmes

Medical Programme Schedule

Number	Course name	Credits
Semester 1		
1	Mathematics B	3
2	Biology volume	2
3	Practical biology volume	1
4	Chemistry volume 1	2
5	General psychology	2
6	Physics B	2
7	Basic English 1	3
8	Basic French 1	3
9	General information technology	2
10	Physical education 1	1
Total, semester 1		18
Semester 2		
11	The NLCB of neo-MLN	5
12	Surgery 1	3
13	Chemistry volume 2	2
14	Practical chemistry	1
15	Basic English 2	2
16	Basic French 2	2
17	Biophysics	2
18	Biophysics practice	1

(continued)

A.G. Shillabeer, *The Health of Vietnam*, DOI 10.1007/978-981-287-709-3

Number	Course name	Credits
19	Medical genetics	3
20	Physical education 2	1
Total, semester 2		20
Semester 3		
21	The military	2
22	Defence work	2
23	General military	2
24	Tactical and technical fire rifles AK	1
25	Basic English 3	2
26	Basic French 3	2
27	Anatomy 2	4
28	Embryonic tissue	4
29	Physiology 1	3
30	Physical education 3	1
31	General immunology	1
32	Occupational exposure to HIV/AIDS	1
Total, semester 3		22
Semester 4		
33	Ho Chi Minh thoughts	2
34	Biochemistry	4
35	Physiology 2	3
36	Microbiology	3
37	Basic nursing	2
38	Psychological medicine – ethics	1
39	Anatomy 3	1
40	Physiology 3	1
41	Skills 1 (communication)	1
42	Skills 2	1
Total, semester 4		17
Semester 5		
43	Pathophysiology	4
44	Parasites	3
45	Pathology	3
46	Diagnostic imaging	2
47	Cabinet base LT	2
48	Cabinet base TH	2
49	Foreign establishments LT	2
50	Foreign establishments TH	1
51	Skills 3 (procedure)	1
52	Skills 4	1
Total, semester 5		20

(continued)

Number	Course name	Credits
Semester 6		
53	Pharmacology	4
54	Surgery practice	2
55	LT general cancer	1
56	General cancer TH	1
57	Education and health promotion	1
58	Health organisation	3
59	Sun Y English	3
60	French S Y	3
61	Community practice I	1
62	Haematology basis	2
63	Research methodology sciences	2
Total, semester 6		18
Semester 7		
64	Internal pathology 1 LT	2
65	Internal pathology 1 TH	2
66	1 LT foreign pathology	2
67	Foreign pathology 1 TH	2
68	Nutrition – FHS	1
69	Statistics and probability	2
70	Obstetrics 1 LT	2
71	Obstetrics 1 TH	2
Total, semester 7		15
Semester 8		
72	Epidemiology	3
73	Environmental science and health environment	3
74	Internal pathology 2 LT	2
75	Internal pathology 2 TH	2
76	Children 1 LT	2
77	Children 1 TH	2
78	The DS BVSKBMTE – v.de RH	1
79	Party lines CM C. VN	3
Total, semester 8		18
Semester 9		
80	1 LT infectious	2
81	1 infectious TH	2
82	Lao LT	1
83	Lao TH	1
84	Rehabilitation LT	1
85	Rehabilitation TH	1
86	Neurology LT	1
87	Neurology TH	1

(continued)

Number	Course name	Credits
88	Mental LT	1
89	Mental TH	1
90	Traditional medicine 1 LT	2
91	Traditional medicine 1 TH	2
92	2 LT infectious	1
93	2 TH infectious	1
94	Traditional medicine 2 LT	1
95	Traditional medicine 2 TH	1
96	Clinical pharmacology LT	1
97	TH clinical pharmacology	1
Total, semester 9		18
Semester 10		
98	National health programme	1
99	Health economics – health insurance	1
100	LT allergies	1
101	Allergy TH	1
102	Oral and maxillofacial LT	1
103	Oral and maxillofacial TH	1
104	Otolaryngology LT	1
105	ENT TH	1
106	Eye LT	1
107	Eyes TH	1
108	LT dermatology	1
109	TH dermatology	1
110	Forensic medicine	2
111	Military medicine	1
112	Community practice II	1
Total, semester 10		16
Semester 11		
113	Internal pathology 3 LT	2
114	Internal pathology 3 TH	2
115	2 LT foreign pathology	2
116	Foreign pathology 2 TH	2
117	Obstetric 2 LT	2
118	Obstetric 2 TH	2
119	Children 2 LT	2
120	Children 2 TH	2
Total, semester 11		16
Semester 12		
121	Thesis	10
122	The final thematic cabinet LT	1
123	The final thematic foreign LT	1
124	The final thematic LT	1

(continued)

Number	Course name	Credits
125	The final thematic paediatric LT	1
126	The final internal TH	4
127	The final foreign TH	4
128	The final product TH	4
129	The final children TH	4
130	The disease is spread through colleges	1
131	Topic LCK secretary	1
132	Topical parasite	1
133	Epidemiology symposium	1
134	Sanitation symposium	1
Total, semester 12		10

LT theory study proportion
LH practical study proportion

Course Content and Level

9.1. KC211005. Mathematics B (3TC, 3-0,0-4). Basic knowledge of limits, continuity and integral calculus functions of one variable; matrix determinants and systems of linear equations; limits, continuity and calculus functions of several variables and integral two layers, three layers, series, functions and differential equations.
9.2. KC211022. Biological CG (2TC, 2-0,0-4). Fundamental characteristic of life and structure and function of the basic units of living cells; processes occurring in living organisms: nutrition, metabolism and transport of material circulation and activity of the endocrine and nervous system, and breeding and genetics.
9.3. KC211023. Practical biology volume (1TC, 0-1,0-2). Principles using a microscope and some forms of cell organelles of animals, plants and microorganisms; water transport across the cell membrane; contractures and reflex contraction of the cytoskeleton; a survey of the phenomenon through the process of cell metabolism and chromosome morphology, the number of chromosomes of an organism.
9.4. KC211018. Chemistry volume 1 (2TC, 2-0,0-4). Knowledge of atomic structure, molecular structure, physical state of aggregation, chemical thermodynamics, kinetic contact effects, chemical reactions and electrical lines.
9.5. SP211014. General psychology (2TC, 2-0,0-2). General psychology presents an overview of the psychological phenomenon; the origin and nature of psychological phenomena and factors affecting the formation and expression of psychological phenomena.
9.6. KC211014. Physics B (2TC, 2-0,0-4). Basic knowledge of mechanical, thermal, electrical, optical and nuclear physics; the law of motion of objects often gawoj in engineering and everyday life; application of laws, the laws of physics to explore and study the interaction between the simple system.

9.7. FL211005. English CB 1 (3TC, 3-0,0-6). To provide a range of vocabulary, structure, grammar and communication skills training at the basic level on topics of normal activities of daily life such as humans and career, job, hobby, transportation, travel, fashion, health and experience. These themes are described and expressed through the medium grammar, language structure and function from categories such as the present form, present continuous, present perfect and past simple, nouns (singular/plural, countable/uncountable, possessive), adverbs, prepositions, adjectives, etc.

9.8. FL211008. French CB 1 (3TC, 3-0,0-6). To provide a range of vocabulary, structure, grammar and communication skills training at the basic level on topics of normal activities of daily life such as humans and career, job, hobby, transportation, travel, fashion, health and experience. These themes are described and expressed through the medium grammar and structure and from categories such as same and, in the present form, present continuous, present perfect and past simple, nouns (singular/plural, countable/uncountable, possessive), adverbs, prepositions, adjectives, etc.

9.9. KC211027. Informatics general (2TC, 1-1). Fundamental concepts of information processing and computers, Internet access operations, the skills used to manipulate the operating system on computers and exploit some application software and storage preparation and serving documents of clerical work. System administrators use database for scientific computing and problem-solving expertise.

9:10. SP211011. Physical education 1(1TC). Course content promulgated in Decision No. 3244/2002/Education and Training and Decision No. 1262/ Education and Training of Ministers dated December 4, 1997 of the Ministry of Education and Training.

9:11. ML211001. The basic principles of Marxism-Leninism (5TC, 3,5-1,5-10). Contents issued Decision No. 52/2008/QD-MoET, dated September 18, 2008, of the Ministry of Education and Training requires political theory to be taught to all students of universities and colleges.

9:12. YD212001. Anatomy 1 (3TC, 2-1). Content covers basic human anatomy, details of organs and systems through theory, models, paintings and other representations of the human body.

9:13. KC211019. Chemistry volume 2 (2TC, 2-0,0-4). Knowledge of the typical non-metals (types of single substances and compounds), the typical metals (pure form and compounds) and the transition metals and structure of organic compounds, hydrocarbons, hydrocarbon derivatives and the derivatives of hydrocarbons.

9:14. KC211021. Practising chemical CG (1TC, 0-1,0-2). Consists of two parts: theory includes qualitative analysis system elements, weight analysis, volumetric analysis and analytical tools and practice includes qualitative analysis of cations, anions, neutral approach, redox method, precipitation method to create complex, determining pH and photometric method.

9:15. FL211006. English CB 2 (2TC, 2 – 0-4). Provides a range of vocabulary, structure, grammar and communication skills training at the basic-level advanced topics such as everyday life, describing appearance, including biography, predicting the future, comparison, etc. These themes are expressed through the medium vocabulary grammatical structures such as verb tenses present/past tense, present/past continuous and present perfect; conditional sentences 1; comparative adjectives; etc.

9:16. FL211009. French CB 2 (2TC, 2 – 0-4). Provides a range of vocabulary, structure, grammar and communication skills training at the basic-level advanced topics such as everyday life, describing appearance, including biography, predicting the future, comparison, etc. These themes are expressed through the medium vocabulary grammar structure as varieties and from the present/past tense, present/past continuous and present perfect, the article event type 1, comparative adjectives, etc.

9:17. KC211016 Biophysics (2TC: 2 – 0.0 to 4). Basic knowledge of physical laws occurring in the organism: the law of carriage of the body material, the potential formation mechanism of biological effects of light and radiation on biological organisms and biophysical processes in a number of specific organs in the organism.

9:18. KC211017. Practice biophysics (1TC: 0 – 1.0 to 2). Testing the learned knowledge of specific experiments, consisting of nine exercises; determination of activation energy of the frog heart contractions; permeability of cells and tissues; durability of the membrane of red blood cells; mobile phones; power authority; and viscosity.

9:19. KC211043. Medical Genetics (3TC, 2-1). Classifications of the human chromosome, the method and genetic research, the research methodology of human chromosomes, the characteristics and mechanisms of common inherited diseases in humans, and the pathology of human chromosomes. The congenital malformations, mechanisms of molecular pathology, significance of genetic pharmacology studies, and principles of diagnosis, treatment, and preventive advice genetics.

9:20. SP211012. Physical education 2 (1TC, 0-1).Course content promulgated in Decision No. 3244/2002/Education and Training and Decision No. 1262/Education and Training dated December 4, 1997, of the Ministry of Education and Training.

9:21. QP211001. QP211002. QP211003. QP211004. Military education (7 TC, 0-7). Contents issued Decision No. 81/2007/QD-MoET, dated December 12, 2007 of the Ministry of Education and Training.

9:22. FL211007. English CB 3 (2TC, 2 – 0-4). Provides some language knowledge on topics such as food and health life, views on jobs, environment, information, jobs, etc. These themes are expressed through the medium vocabulary grammar structures such as verb tenses present/past simple, ongoing, completed, conditional sentences two and three, passive/active structure, etc. and practise communication skills with language proficiency at the advanced level, as a basis for reading and studying English literature in the field of expertise.

9:23. FL211010. French CB 3 (2TC, 2 – 0-4). Provides some language knowledge on topics such as food and health, attitudes towards employment, environment, information belief, etc. These themes are expressed through the medium vocabulary grammar structures such as verb tenses present/past simple, ongoing, pre-past, conditional sentences two and three, structured passive/active, etc. and practise communication skills with language proficiency at the advanced level, as a basis for reading and study French literature in the field of expertise.

9:24. YD212002. Anatomy 2 (four credits, 2-2). Structure, location, relevance and functioning of the human body in normal and pathological, people in total harmony relationship with the environment, people are always in a state of mobilisation, innovation and constant interaction between the environment on human health.

9:25. YD212004. Embryonic tissue (3TC, 2-1). Structure morphology in normal presentation including, molecules of tissues, organs in the body; identifying tissues, organs and their structures in detail using an optical microscope; the formation and normal development of the human from fertilisation through nuclear development stages; the origin of the generation, normal development; structure and function of the parts of the human embryo; THE formation of a number of common congenital malformations.

9:26. YD212006. Physiology 1 (3TC, 2-1). Functions and operational functions of the organs and organ systems in the body; regulatory mechanisms and function of organs and organ systems to ensure consistency between the body and the environment.

9:27. SP211013. Physical Education 3 (1TC, 0-1). Course content promulgated in Decision No. 3244/2002/Education and Training and Decision No. 1262/ Education and Training dated April 12, 1997 of the Ministry of Education and Training.

9:28. YD212017. General Immunology (1TC, 1-0). Introductory immunology, immune response and antigen recognition molecules of antigen-antibody; some effects of system T cells and plasma. Agencies involved cell immune response.

9:29. YD212018. Occupational exposure to HIV/AIDS (1TC, 1-0).

9:30. ML211002. Ho Chi Minh Thoughts (2TC: 1.5 to 0.5 – 4). Contents issued Decision No. 52/2008/QD-MoET, dated September 9, 2008, by the Ministry of Education and Training requires political theory teaching for all students of universities and colleges.

Prerequisite: the basic principles of Marxism-Leninism

9:31. YD212005. Biochemistry (four credits, 3-1). Structure and metabolism of cells mainly in the living body, the relationship and regulatory mechanisms of cells and tissues, the biological catalyst and bioenergy occurring in vivo. Some conventional tests.

9:32. YD212007. Physiology 2 (3TC, 2-1). Explore technology to enable diagnosis, treatment and the application of physiology knowledge in a clinical setting.

9:33. YD212011. Microbiology (3TC, 2-1). Associate microorganisms, infection, antibiotic resistance and the students; virulence factors of microorganisms; the body's resistance to pathogenic microorganisms and bacteria, viruses and pathogenic organisms in humans.

9:34. YD212012. Basic nursing (2TC, 1-1). Understand and practice standard techniques for monitoring and care of patients in a hospital setting.

9.35. YD212013. Psychological medicine – ethics (1TC, 1-0). Fundamental concepts in psychology; the importance of the psychological impact on health; the types of psychological characteristics of the age; the mood swings typical of psychological illness; the basic skills when exposed to patients, communities and colleagues in professional practice; moral qualities characteristic of the practising physician and the medical research.

9:36. YD212003. Anatomy 3 (1TC, 1-0). The anatomic landmarks in a number of surgical procedures, obstetric and related specialist; some situations cause complications to surgery in some areas of the body; application of anatomical knowledge to diagnosis and treatment as well as serving basis to other subjects.

9:37. YD212008. Physiology 3 (1TC, 1-0). Particular characteristics of the function of organs and organ systems in the body of some ethnic groups in the central highlands, regulatory mechanisms of function of organs and organ systems to ensure unity between the body and environment of some ethnic groups in the central highlands and applying the knowledge of the characteristics of the organs and organ systems of a number of ethnic groups in the central highlands of classes in clinical medicine.

9:38. YD212023. Skills 1 (communication) (1TC, 0-1).

9:39. YD212024. Skills 2 (1TC, 0-1).

9:40. YD212014. Pathophysiology and immunology (four credits, 3-1). Develop an understanding of, the main function of organs, systems, common disease states; the pathogenesis of the condition to support the diagnosis therapy, addiction argued review and consultation; some common disorder in actual clinical use; the body's response in antimicrobial immunity.

9.41. YD212015. Parasites (3TC, 2-1). Understand physiology and ecology of parasites that cause disease and infection in Viet Nam. Harmful effects of common parasites in our country; the epidemiological characteristics of parasitic diseases in Viet Nam; the biological characteristics, epidemiology, prevention and control of parasitic diseases of animals; the diagnostic methods parasitic diseases and the principles and measures against parasitic diseases.

9:42. YD212016. Surgical patient management (3TC, 2-1). Fundamental knowledge about the morphological changes of cells and tissues in the disease process; identifying the relationship between morphology and function in the analysis of the clinical manifestations of the disease; and using the results of diagnostic biopsy and cytology for diagnosis of the disease is common in South Viet Nam.

9:43. YD212021. Diagnostic imaging (2TC, 1-1). Common diseases common in the X-ray film with typical pathological images, principles of imaging techniques in modern medicine and the strengths and weaknesses of diagnostic methods in medical imaging.

9:44. Medicine D213031. YD213032. Civil basis (four credits, 2-2). Cardiovascular physical examination. The heart sounds normal and pathological. Subclinical cardiovascular system and clinical examination of respiratory system. Subclinical respiratory difficulty in breathing, coughing up blood and pus. The unusual sound when listening to the lungs and clinical examination in the digestive system. Subclinical digestive system and clinical examination and urinary system. Subclinical urinary system and clinical examination of the endocrine system. Subclinical endocrine system and clinical examination of the musculoskeletal system. Subclinical musculoskeletal system: patient method. The syndrome of heart failure. Syndrome, pneumothorax; syndrome, pleural effusion; pulmonary syndrome typical coagulation; ascites syndrome; jaundice syndrome; constipation; back pain; haematuria syndrome; syndrome, shortness of breath; and syndrome, consistent.

9:45. YD213033. YD213034. Offline basis (3TC, 2-1). Disease surgical plan. Surgical abdominal examination; detailed examination of the spine and pelvis; symptomatology fractures, joints; discover the urinary system and the male reproductive system; discover injuries, chest injuries; examination of blood vessels and peripheral nerves; discover injury, traumatic brain injury; sterile, surgical sterilisation; rectal examination, the rectum; general anaesthesia and general anaesthesia. Associate of burns; syndrome, increased intracranial pressure; peritonitis syndrome; intestinal obstruction syndrome. Syndrome: bleeding; obstructive jaundice syndrome; cord compression syndrome; symptomatic carbuncle, juniors, abscesses and nine edge.

9:46. YD212025. Skills 3 (TIP) (1TC, 0-1).

9:47. YD212026. Skills 4 (1TC, 0-1).

9:48. YD212019. Pharmacology (four credits, 3-1). Fundamental knowledge on the pharmacokinetics and pharmacodynamics of the drug classes used in clinical practice.

9:49. YD212020. Surgery practice (2TC, 1-1). The basic movements in general surgery on animals. These are some basic surgical emergency surgery normally.

9:50. YD213035. YD213036. General cancer (2TC, 1-1). Causes of cancer, the natural history of cancer, the detection and diagnosis of cancer, rating and ranking of clinical pathology of cancer and the methods of treating cancer.

9:51. YD212029. Education and health promotion (1TC, 1-0). Associate in health education (health education), the basic concepts of health education, the purpose of health education – process of behaviour change –the principle of health education in the health education group at the base and planning, implementing, evaluating a health education programme.

9:52. YD213087. WHO (3TC, 2-1). Associate of healthcare organisations; health strategy and the objectives of the health sector in 2002; law to protect people's health, Viet Nam; primary healthcare; health management; Viet Nam's health system; organisation and management of health facilities; Health plan; operating, monitoring and evaluation of health activities; statistical indicators of health – illness – and evaluation of primary healthcare in the primary healthcare online.

9:53. FL213011. Specialisation in English (3TC, 3-0). Gives students the technical term care sector, helping students to read, understand documents and access information and new materials in English more easily and is then applied to the process of learning and professional studies students.

9:54. FL213015. Specialisation in French (3TC, 3-0). Gives students the technical term care sector, helping students to read, understand documents and access information and new materials in French easier and is then applied to the process of learning and professional studies students.

9:55. YD212030. Community practice I (1TC, 0-1). Based on what the students learned after 3 years, in addition to the basic subjects, students have been learning about: education and health promotion and health organisations. So, in the field, mainly students practise skills: outreach, conducted health education to the people and learn about the health system organisations at the grass roots.

9:56. YD212010. Methodology of Science (2TC, 2-0).

9:57. YD212009. Haematology basis (2TC, 2-0.) Basic theory of haematology and blood transfusion; looking at the division of haematology subjects: blood transfusions such as cells, coagulation, immunology, genetics and blood transfusion; and application techniques of haematology tests – blood transfusion to reality.

9:58. YD213037. YD213038. Civil pathology 1 (four credits, 2-2). Diagnosis, treatment and counselling are a number of common medical conditions; assessment and initial management of common emergency diseases: circulatory system (diagnosis and management of chest pain, angina, myocardial infarction, chronic heart discarded and respiratory system management of pneumothorax, lung cancer).

9:59. YD213043. YD213044. Secretary pathology 1 (four credits, 2-2). Diagnosis and aid some surgical patients; move the patient to a higher level of treatment in special time; the exchange of generalised disease: inflammation of appendicitis, bowel obstruction, intussusception, infection of the peritoneum, chest injuries, urinary system injuries, pyloric stenosis, gastric perforation, rupture of solid organs, andcancer.

9.60. YD212022. Nutrition – hygiene and food safety (1TC, 1-0). Chemical composition, nutritional value and the principles of hygiene and common diseases in every kind of food; roles and nutrient needs related to health and illness of the human body; propaganda for people in the community about issues on nutrition and food safety, given the preventive measures, and the importance of nutrition for health and human disease.

9.61. KC211006. Probability and statistics (3TC, 3-0). The basic knowledge of probability, events, probability of events and the nature of probability; random, discrete and continuous variables: expectation and variance; the basic types of distribution, distribution binomial, Poisson, exponential, standard, etc.; law of large numbers and limit theorems; theoretical estimation and hypothesis testing and regression and correlation.

9.62. YD213047. YD213048. Obstetrics 1 (four credits, 2-2). Issues of obstetrics course: production facility, physiology and gynaecology; normal pregnancy; real difficulty, anddifficult birth causes – diagnosis and management.

9.63. YD212028. Epidemiology (3TC, 2-1). Epidemiology in general; applied epidemiology: strategies for epidemiologic studies, descriptive epidemiology, epidemiological analysis, epidemiological intervention; the epidemiology of infectious diseases, the process of translation, the epidemiology of the disease is spread through the respiratory tract, the epidemiology of gastrointestinal diseases, the epidemiology of diseases transmitted through blood, the epidemiology of transmitted diseases in the mucocutaneous zone, community diagnosis and screening to detect disease in the community series.

9.64. YD212027. Environmental science and environmental health (3TC, 2-1). Biological and environmental population and community ecology environment; environment health and population and ecosystem agriculture energy and environmental pollution; water sanitation and supply of clean water, schools; the school-related diseases; hygiene urban residential areas, hospitals, air pollution, soil environment; general medical burden on labour and employment; the principles of preventive occupational hazards; the occupational hazards due to biological factors, adverse effects due to the physical elements of the production process; toxicology and occupational disease prevention and control measures; pesticides, herbicides, rodenticides, the poison gas and dust ergonomic precautions – diseases caused by dust in the manufacturing process.

9.65. YD213039. YD213040. Civil pathology 2 (four credits, 2-2). The digestive system (chronic hepatitis, cirrhosis, liver abscess, irritable bowel syndrome, constipation); endocrine system (diabetes, Graves, simple goitre); blood (diagnosis and treatment of anaemia, leukaemia level, economic leukaemia) and urinary tract (acute renal failure, glomerulonephritis levels, urinary bladder inflammation.

9.66. YD213051. YD213052. Paediatrics 1 (four credits, 2-2). Paediatric basis: physiological characteristic anatomical organs in children; the period of youth, mental development, advocacy, children's physical; programmes in child healthcare.

9.67. YD213085. VD population, the health protection BMTE – reproductive health (1TC, 1-0). Demography; consulting services in family planning; reproductive health education for minors; family planning and maternal and child health.

9.68. ML211003. Revolutionary policy of the Communist Party of South Viet Nam (3TC). Contents issued Decision No. 52/2008/QD-MoET, dated September 18, 2008, of the Ministry of Education and Training plans to hold teaching political theory courses for student members of universities and colleges.

Prerequisite: Ho Chi Minh Thoughts

9.69. YD213055. YD213056. Infectious diseases 1 (four credits, 2-2). Definition, characteristics and classification of infectious diseases; diagnostic criteria, causes and management of infectious diseases through the blood and skin and mucosa; methods of preventing blood-borne diseases and mucocutaneous; disease transmission through the digestive tract and respiratory tract; treatment principle, the common complications, treatment for complications of gastrointestinal and respiratory precautionary principle transmitted diseases. Khang biotherapy of infectious diseases; use of corticosteroids in infectious diseases.

9.70. YD213067. YD213068. Lao (2TC, 1-1). Pulmonary TB (HIV); TB treatment; characteristics and current situation of tuberculosis; National TB Control Programme; tuberculosis; tuberculosis infection profile, tuberculosis meningitis, peritoneal TB, bone and joint TB, TB nodes; Urinary tuberculosis and pleural genital TB.

9.71. YD213077. YD213078. Rehabilitation (2TC, 1-1). Process and prevent disability; rehabilitation (rehab) based on the community; the secondary injury, detection and prevention; outline of the methods of commonly used physical therapy; overview of rehabilitation techniques; an examination of people with disabilities; manual muscle test; measurement of joint range; practise manipulating devices for rehabilitation; role of physical therapy (physiotherapy), rehabilitation of the physically handicapped; role of physiotherapy, rehabilitation of mental disability; role of physiotherapy, rehabilitation and disability in most severe disabilities; rehabilitation for patients with hemiplegia; rehabilitation for patients with spinal cord injury.

9.72. YD213079. YD213080. Neurology (2TC, 1-1). Recalling some anatomical, neurological function; hemiplegia syndrome; syndrome legs; increased intracranial pressure; seizures; cerebral vascular accident; several methods of subclinical nerve; encephalitis syndrome; second hip pain and coma.

9.73. YD213081. YD213082. Psychiatry (2TC, 1-1). Associate and psychiatric symptoms; drug addiction; alcohol abuse and alcoholism; mental disorder actual damage; schizophrenia; depression; stress-related disorders; agitation; suicide and mental healthcare in the community.

9.74. YD213057. YD213058. Traditional Medicine 1 (four credits, 2-2). traditional and brief history of our Party's view of traditional medicine today; theory of Yin and Yang; five elements theory; four diagnostic – bat diamond; eight principles of treatment methods; using the usually grave; acupuncture and traditional medicine. Some remedies are often used in traditional medicine.

9.75. YD213059. YD213060. Infectious diseases 2 (2TC, 1-1.) Use of corticosteroids in infectious diseases; antimalarial drugs; treatment of bacterial meningitis, malaria and dengue shock; retroviral drugs and how to use; treatment of drug-resistant typhoid, hepatitis malignancy and chronic hepatitis.

9.76. YD213061. YD213062. 2 Traditional medicine (2TC, 1-1). Rheumatoid arthritis; neck and shoulder pain; sciatica; VII nerve paralysis peripheral; flu – method wind; depression; peptic ulcers; cerebral vascular accident; treatment of dengue (level I, II) by traditional medicine; acupressure massage.

9.77. YD213063. YD213064. Clinical pharmacology (2TC, 1-1).

9.78. YD213084. National Health Programme (1TC, 1-0). Expanded programme on immunisation; the prevention of iodine deficiency disorders; the S/FP/RH; malaria control programmes; programme prevention of malnutrition; programme prevention of diarrhoea; programme on HIV/AIDS; leprosy control programmes.

9.79. YD213086. Health economics – healthcare insurance (1TC, 1-0). Associate economy; health economics, the relationship between economics and health; applied health economics in health services; financial health, management applications in financial basis; general health insurance (HI); system organisation and operation of health insurance; the policies related to the state's health insurance in Viet Nam; the basic content of health insurance and the process of health insurance operations.

9.80. YD213065. YD213066. Allergies (2TC, 1-1). Some basic concepts and modern allergy immunity; allergens; anaphylaxis and anaphylactic shock; bronchial asthma; allergies; autoimmune diseases; allergic rhinitis; the specific method of diagnosing allergies; the specific treatment of allergic disease; urticaria – Quincke's oedema and dermatitis, contact dermatitis.

9.81. YD213069. YD213070. Dentistry (2TC, 1-1). Disease cavities; pulp inflammation; inflammation around the tooth stem; gingivitis and periodontal inflammation; inflammation of connective tissue and maxillofacial region; emergency jaw and facial injuries, and regular dental; trauma to the hand function; tooth extraction, tooth extraction contraindications, complications associated with systemic oral; co-infection of the mediastinum; congenital malformation of the maxillofacial region; maxillofacial region tumours (benign + malignant);and dental care in the community.

9.82. YD213071. YD213072. Otolaryngology (2TC, 1-1). Opening theme; symptomatology ear, mastoid; symptoms of sinusitis school; symptomatology of the throat, vocal; otitis media, inflammation of the ear bones; the major intracranial complications caused by the ear; rhinitis, sinusitis face; sore throat, tonsils – VA. Oesophageal foreign bodies – foreign body airway; bleeding from the nose; following a throat abscess and nasopharyngeal cancer (NPC).

9.83. YD213073. YD213074. Eyes (2TC, 1-1). again anatomy and physiology of visual-related eye diseases; diagnosing the cause of red eye; diagnosing the cause of blurred vision; glaucoma disease – pressure labels – market; disease conjunctivitis; trachoma; disease uveitis; disease and ulcerative keratitis cornea; visual acuity and refractive error; cataracts and eye injuries, burns in the eyes.

9.84. YD213075. YD213076. Dermatology (2TC, 1-1). Lesions, basic; skin toxicity due to drugs, cosmetics; atopic dermatitis; contact dermatitis; eczema fat; scabies; disease moment; shingles; chickenpox; herpes; psoriasis; tinea; gonorrhoea; syphilis; nongonococcal urethritis disease; management methods for STD patients with TC and HC; mucocutaneous manifestations of HIV/AIDS and leprosy.

9.85. YD213083. Forensic medicine (2TC, 1-1). Associate of forensic medicine – school corpses; injury legal medicine; toxicology forensic medicine; genital forensic medicine; suffocated: causes carbon oxide inhalation in animals; water to suffocate animals; asphyxiation by hanging animals and tabulation expertise – commercial licence.

9.86. YD212088. Military medicine (1TC, 0-1). Responsibilities and obligations of every citizen in the national defence, especially the specialised knowledge related to the service of defence of health workers; performing some anti-war engineering chemistry, microbiology and some knowledge of internal medicine, surgery field, initial emergency for the wounded and knowing how to deploy troops Y field stations in the field.

9.87. YD212089. 2 Community practice (1TC, 0-1). Examination and diagnosis is the basis of common human diseases; establish disease patterns in community internships; join the national health program; investigation, review and analysis of data 1 issue of environmental sanitation, a medical epidemiologist or a National Health Programme.

9.88. YD213041. YD213042. Civil pathology 3 (four credits, 2-2). Nervous system (diagnosis and management of coma, emergency cerebral vascular accident, headache); resuscitation (shock, emergency circulatory respiratory arrest, haemoptysis emergency, electric shock, water asphyxia, snakebite, management of acute poisoning, toxicity levels often); elderly pathology and diagnosis and management of back pain.

9.89. YD213045. YD213046. Secretary pathology 2 (four credits, 2-2). Exchange of injuries and diseases: diagnosis and aid of fracture and closed and open dislocations of the upper limb and lower limb; first aid vascular injuries, burns; diagnosis and early detection chamber tamponade; blood by fat embolism in fracture.

9.90. YD213049. YD213050. Obstetrics 2 (four credits, 2-2). Production diseases: lessons of the disease – diagnosis and management; gynaecology, the all gynaecological disease, diagnosis and management; family planning and reproductive healthcare.

9.91. YD213053. YD213054. Paediatrics 2 (four credits, 2-2). Pathology paediatric symptoms: the disease is common in children; how to detect and manage care; paediatric treatment, the syndrome, first aid and disaster and how to treat drug use in children.

9.92. YD216090. Graduation thesis (ten credits). Carry, implement and protect the content thesis: the theme of internal medicine, surgical, obstetrics, paediatrics, infectious, etc.; regarding public health and a number of specialised other sectors.

9.93. YD216091. Specialist subject LT final (1TC, 1-0).

9.94. YD216092. Thematic LT foreign final (1TC, 1-0).

9.95. YD216093. Thematic LT final product (1TC, 1-0).

9.96. YD216094. Paediatric symposium final LT (1TC, 1-0).

9.97. YD216095. Civil TH final (four credits, 0-4).

9.98. YD216096. Secretary TH final (four credits, 0-4).

9.99. YD216097. TH final product (four credits, 0-4).

9100. YD216098. Paediatrics final TH (four credits, 0-4).

9101. YD216099. Thematic diseases transmitted sexually (1TC, 1-0). Syndromes and common diseases transmitted sexually and the treatment regimen and preventive measures.

9102. YD216099. LCK foreign symposium (1TC, 1-0). Provision for common diseases: dentistry, eyes and ENT community.
9103. YD216100. Parasitology symposium (1TC, 1-0). Disease parasite transmitted from animals to humans: diagnosis, treatment and prevention.
9104. YD216101. Epidemiology symposium (1TC, 1-0).
9105. YD216102. Sanitation symposium (1TC, 1-0).

Appendix B

Full table of health indicators and trends

#	Indicator	Year 2009	2011	2015	Criteria
1	Life expectancy (years)	72.8	73.0	74.0	B, C, H
	(Male)	70.2	70.4	N/A	–
	(Female)	75.6	75.8	N/A	–
2	Total fertility rate (childbearing-age women)	2.03	1.99	1.86	B
3	Reduction in fertility (annual %)	–0.9	0.5	0.1	B, C, H
4	Population growth (%)	1.06	1.04	0.93	B, C, H
5	Population (millions)	86.0	87.8	<92	B, C, H
6	Maternal mortality ratio (per 100,000 live births)	69.0	67	58.3	B, C, D, H
7	Infant mortality rate (per 1000 live births)	16.0	15.5	14.8	B, C, D, H
8	<5 years mortality rate (per 1000 live births)	24.1	23.3	19.3	B, C, D, H
9	Malnutrition rate <5 years (% underweight)	18.9	16.8	15.0	A, B, C, H
10	Malnutrition rate <5 years (% stunting)	31.9	27.5	26.0	B, C, H
11	Doctors (per 10,000 people)	6.59	7.23	8.0	C, H
12	Commune health stations with a doctor (%)	67.7	71.9	80	B, C, H
13	Commune health stations with ob/gyn expertise (%)	95.7	95.3	>95	A, B, C, H
14	Villages with a health worker (%)	75.8	82.9	90	B, C, H
15	Public share of total health spending (%)	42.2	N/A	>50	C, H
16	Health insurance coverage (%)	58.2	64.9	80	B, C, H
17	Catastrophic out-of-pocket health cost (%)	5.5	N/A	N/A	–
18	Hospital beds (per 10,000)	20.2	N/A	23	B, C, H
19	Communes meeting health benchmarks (%)	65.4	N/A	60	C, H
20	TB detection rate (per 100,000)	52.2	57.7	N/A	
21	HIV prevalence (per 100,000)	187	224.4	<300	B, C, H
22	Dengue detection (per 100,000)	122	N/A	N/A	B

(continued)

A.G. Shillabeer, *The Health of Vietnam*, DOI 10.1007/978-981-287-709-3

#	Indicator	Year			Criteria
		2009	2011	2015	
23	Smoking prevalence (% age 16+)	N/A	N/A (47.4 in 2010)	N/A	B
24	Low birth weight (%)	5.3	N/A	N/A	B, C, D, H
25	Immunisation <1 year (%)	96.3	96	>90	–
26	Pregnancies with >3 antenatal visits (%)	N/A	82.6	80	D, F
27	Skilled assisted deliveries (%)	94.4	97.2	96	D, F
28	Birth sex ratio (M/100F)	111	111.9	<113	B, C, H
29	Medical facilities with waste treatment (%)	74	N/A	80	A, H
30	University-trained pharmacists (per 10,000 population)	1.77	N/A	1.8	C, H
31	Health workers with licence (%)	0	0	400	–
32	Health spending as % GDP	6.6	N/A	N/A	–
33	Per capita health spending (1000 VND)	159.9	N/A	N/A	–
34	Out-of-pocket share (%)	50.5	N/A	N/A	–
35	Inpatient spending per user over a year (1000 VND)	2097	N/A	N/A	–
36	Outpatient spending per user over a year (1000 VND)	640	N/A	N/A	–
37	Substandard drugs (per 10,000 tests)	330	N/A	N/A	–
38	Retail pharmacies (per 10,000 people)	4.9	N/A	N/A	–
39	Blood units screened for 5 infectious diseases prior to transfusion (%)	N/A	N/A	100	–
40	Inpatient admissions per year (per 100 people)	13.3	N/A	N/A	–
41	Outpatient visits per year (per 100 people)	37.7	N/A	N/A	–
42	People with hospital contacts with health or exemption card (%)	N/A	N/A (66.7, 2010)	N/A	–
43	Inpatient admission duration (days)	6.9	6.8	N/A	–
44	TB cure rate (per 100,000 people)	90.6	90.8	N/A	–
45	Malaria incidence (per 100,000 people)	70.8	N/A	N/A (15 by 2020)	–
46	Leprosy prevalence (per 100,000 people)	0.04	N/A	0.20	–
47	Leprosy detection (per 100,000 people)	0.41	0.37	0.30	–
48	HIV incidence (per 100,000 people)	16.1	16.1	N/A	–
49	Mental health service in communes (%)	63.8	N/A	N/A	–
50	Diagnosed hypertension in treatment (%)	N/A	N/A	N/A	–
51	Diagnosed diabetes in treatment (%)	N/A	N/A	N/A	–
52	Women over 40 screened for breast cancer (%)	N/A	N/A	20	–
53	Food poisoning (People)	5212	4700	N/A	–
	(Incidents)	152	148	N/A	–
	(Deaths)	35	27	N/A	–

(continued)

#	Indicator	Year			Criteria
		2009	2011	2015	
54	Pregnant women having 2+ tetanus vaccinations (%)	93.7	94.5	N/A	–
55	Postpartum care within 42 days (%)	81.9	87.7	85	–
56	Total receiving postpartum care (%)	81.9	85	N/A	F
57	Contraceptive use prevalence (%)	N/A	78.2	100	D
58	Households with improved latrine (%)	48	55	65	–
59	Households with improved drinking water (%)	79	78	85	–

Key to criteria:
A National Assembly indicator assigned to the health sector
B Government indicator assigned to the GSO and MOH for data
C Indicator in the 6-year health sector plan
D Millennium Development Goal
E WHO recommendation
F Indicator in the national health target programme
H National strategy for the protection, care and promotion of people's health 2011–2020
HPG Health Partnership Group
GSO General Statistics Office
MOH Ministry of Health
NHA National Health Accounts
NN National Institute of Nutrition
NTP National Target Programme

Appendix C

A.G. Shillabeer, *The Health of Vietnam*, DOI 10.1007/978-981-287-709-3

JANS comments on the process and content of the 2010–2015 health plan final draft

Dimensions and attributes	Comments on process and content	Recommendations
Dimension 1 Situation analysis and programming		
Attribute 1 National strategy is based on a sound situational and response analysis of the context	**Participation**: There has clearly been a great effort on the part of MOH to better integrate the Joint Annual Health Report (JAHR) and the plan. The plan has successfully identified a number of important issues to be covered. Analysis and inputs for the plan are more comprehensive and participatory than previous plan 2006–2010	Despite significant progress, whilst maintaining stronger participation by existing stakeholders, expansions to others are important and ensure relevance, e.g. Social Committee of the National Assembly, consumer representatives, professional groups, private sector, education and other relevant sectors, representatives from grass-roots levels
Attribute characteristic 1.1 The situation analysis is based on a comprehensive and participatory analysis of health determinants and health outcome trends within the context of the country	Key informants endorse strong participation and engagement by stakeholders in producing JAHR: DPF together with JAHR working group developed JAHR report framework and organised workshop with participation by HPG. Various departments of MOH and related stakeholders provide comments, recruit national consultants for each specific areas of JAHR, write up a report and organise three workshops to get comments (one WS discussed the difficulties, constraints and challenges of healthcare system; one discussed on priority setting for the next 5 years and one on identification of solutions and interventions)	
	Various departments of MOPH also contribute to the situation assessment, though they describe situation of their routine works but not focused on problem identifications and other health system context. It is one of difficulties that the planning team has to face with	
	After three workshops between planning team and JAHR teams, there were increased linkages and dialogues. Especially the JAHR WS on setting priorities, outputs from WS were sent immediately to the planning group. Vice versa, the outputs of the WS organised by the planning group on solutions were fed back to JAHR team. In the workshop, indicators were identified which are appropriate with both priorities identified in JAHR and objectives of 5-year health plan	

	Comprehensiveness: JAHR furnishes based on (i) assessed current situation; (ii) identified priorities of the health sectors and (iii) support for developing annual health sector plan. Annual JAHR exercise focuses each year on thematic topics. JAHR 2010 aims to provide inputs for the development of the plan, and it looks at 6 health systems building blocks	Analysis of determinants could be improved considerably based on existing studies and surveys. Understanding the actual cause behind those indicators and determinants is important and will be helpful in justifying planned interventions
	However, analysis of indicators and determinants is still not comprehensive enough to show the actual causes behind those indicators and determinants. For example, the analysis shows there are large disparities between regions in some of indicators such as IMR and child malnutrition but did not assess the reasons for that. Similarly for analysis of health determinants, it focuses on listing health determinants but not much on pointing out their root causes such as social, cultural, economic and especially organisational/system context	It is necessary to demonstrate geographical disparities and its causes of MMR for specific interventions in the plan
		Health determinants: comprehensive analysis of physical and social-cultural-economic, ethnicity, education, gender determinants. Note that injuries and accidents are health outcomes, not determinants
Attribute characteristic 1.2 The analysis uses disaggregated data to describe progress towards achieving overall health sector policy objectives in line with the policy dimensions of resolution WHA 2009 62.12 on primary healthcare: universal coverage, to improve health equity; service delivery, to make health systems people centred; public policies, to promote and protect the health of communities; leadership, to make health authorities more reliable	Draft 3 did not adequately describe progresses towards achieving overall health sector policy objectives in line with the policy dimensions of resolution on PHC	Need to be added in draft 4, though some parts are reflected in the human resources development

(continued)

Dimensions and attributes	Comments on process and content	Recommendations
Attribute characteristic 1.3 Identification of priority problem areas and programmatic gaps	Priority problems and solutions are identified separately by specific areas	It would be important for the situation analysis to better prioritise key issues to be addressed
	The causes of those priority problems are not well assessed in the situation section. It is necessary to look at specific problems in the context of health system to devise specific and effective policy interventions	Among the seven building blocks [pharmaceutical and vaccines are separate item from the medical equipment] and three other issues in section 12, what are the priority and major entry points, given that resource might not be available to address all of them?
	Though a number of key issues have been identified, HPG suggests there should be a stronger interrelationship and interactions across different key issues	
	The lack of integration across different areas (partly as a result of financing flows to different subsectors) represents one of the major weaknesses in the health system, in large part due to the fact that a number of vertical programmes are operating in parallel with each other and are not well integrated in terms of implementation as well as management. As Viet Nam has reached middle-income-country status, these issues will become increasingly important over the next 5 years. As donor funding to health starts to decline, it is important for the government to consider ways in which efficiency can be improved	
	Where some programmes still do not achieve indicators as targeted, it is necessary to analyse reasons for that of which referring to its implementation	
	Section 12 describes the priority issues to be addressed, the plan proposed 10 areas, seven out of ten are health systems building blocks and three other health issues, namely, family planning, health status and disparities and preventive medicines at primary healthcare level, are highlighted. It is unclear how these were prioritised. There is no clear process on the priority setting	

Attribute 2 Clearly defined priority areas, goals, objectives, interventions and expected outcomes that contribute to improve health outcomes and meeting national and global commitment		
Attribute characteristic 1.4 Objectives are measurable, realistic and time bound	The objective described in draft 3 is rather general. The objective is too broad and includes, to reduce morbidity and mortality, promote health and increase life expectancy, improve the quality of our race, contribute to improving the quality of life and the quality of the human resources and foster the formation of a synchronised system of healthcare from the central to the grass- roots levels and people's habit of keeping good health, in response to the needs of industrialisation, modernisation, national building and defences	It is necessary to provide specific objectives of the plan of which measurable, realistic and time-bound criteria need to be taken into consideration, although the target to achieve by 2015 is clearly written in the table under section 3 on basic health indicators
	It is felt that the objectives and target indicators by 2015 are realistic; however, hospital bed per 10,000 inhabitants (exclude CHS bed) would increase from 20.5 to 23.0; this means around 21,000 new beds would put in place by 2015. There is a need to ensure that this target is realistic	There is a need to plan for adequate number of health workers to operate these beds and retain them in public health sector. It is not clear on what are the policy interventions on rural retention and increase enrolment of new graduates in rural health services
	The reduction in MMR from 68 in 2010 to 58.3 by 2015 needs a statement that this would be achievable	
	It would be extremely difficult to increase population coverage on insurance from 60 % in 2010 to 80 % in 2015 due to nature of the contributory scheme for the informal sector despite the high level of budget subsidies	

(continued)

Dimensions and attributes	Comments on process and content	Recommendations
Attribute characteristic 1.5 Goals, objectives and interventions address health priorities, equitable access and quality and health outcomes across all population subgroups, especially vulnerable groups	Goal, objectives, results and key interventions are not well structured. It is not clear how prioritisation was done, what strategies and specific interventions will be carried out and how they will respond to the needs of vulnerable groups (age, gender, wealth, urban/rural). Also, it is not clear what effective interventions would be chosen to meeting national/global commitments	It is necessary to address health priorities, equitable access and quality and health outcomes across all population subgroups, especially vulnerable groups in the objectives and interventions
	Though a number of priority areas are identified, these remain broad and seemingly cover the range of interventions included in the plan. Subsequently, interventions are not systematically organised and appear to be a listing of existing/planned *projects/ programmes in the sector.* This is because the situation analysis does not provide sufficient in-depth analysis in certain key areas; therefore, the real cause of the problem is often not considered in a systematic way	It should better focus the perspective of patient-centred care and linked with this a more holistic approach to PHC, for example, the development of patient right or charter and empowerment of consumer protection groups
		DPF should include intervention to improve health governance and support MOH and its subnational system and strengthen capacity to undertake more and better its stewardship role
	Although there is no systematic burden of disease study in Viet Nam, routine statistics shows that chronic NCD is increasingly a major problem of disease and economic burden. Unfortunately, there is no priority programme to address the chronic NCD. References on cost-effective clinical and community-based interventions should be referred from the DCP2	Suggest that influenza, rabies, cholera and acute watery diarrhoea are added under the section on preventive medicine. Also suggest a specific reference to preparedness for complex public health emergencies including pandemics and strengthening disease surveillance and co-ordination between human and animal health. At the end of the section on preventive medicine, suggest adding a sentence on multi-sector co-ordination on complex health issues, including multi-sector pandemic preparedness

	There is a sporadic reference to chronic obstructive pulmonary disease which is attributable to tobacco use. There is a need to address how Viet Nam would bring down prevalence of regular smoker and better protect the health of the non-smokers and enforce a smoke-free environment	A new priority programme on effective intervention to prevent and control chronic NCD should be provided
	Although the need to improve primary healthcare is described, there appears to be no clear strategy concerning how this will be done. For example, there is no reference to the linkages/ interaction between different levels of care (especially primary and secondary), in order to offer a comprehensive package of care to the population (particularly those disadvantaged groups) and ensure proper referral backup services at the provincial level or how to make patient-centred care as well as how to make healthcare becomes universal coverage	
	Due to lack of in-depth analysis of the context in identifying causes of priority problems and programmatic gaps, therefore, there are no specific programmes to improve health governance and support MOH and its subnational system to strengthen capacity to undertake more and better stewardship role when it is seen as crucial in the next 5 years. This also includes more detailed activities in strengthening the legal framework	
	The private sector has been touched on briefly, but no specific or concrete programmes/interventions to harness the potential of private sector in healthcare (other than a relatively general statement on developing mechanisms to strengthen collaboration with the private sector). Careful management of the growing magnitude of the private sector is so critical in various dimension, e.g. universal coverage, human resource migration dynamics, inefficiency and potential supplier-induced demands and catastrophic health expenditure to the households	

(continued)

Dimensions and attributes	Comments on process and content	Recommendations
Attribute 3 'Planned intervention is feasible, locally appropriate, equitable and based on evidence and good practice, including consideration of effectiveness and sustainability'		
Attribute characteristic 1.6 Planned strategies and interventions are based upon analysis of effectiveness and impact and clearly identify how they contribute to expected results	Planned strategies and interventions are not clearly reflecting that they are based on analysis of effectiveness and impact. There is no reference how these interventions contribute to expected outcomes	Given there are a number of programmes that have been implemented over the last 5 years and these programmes are found to be implemented again in this plan without specificity of whether or not they are truly effective and necessary to be maintained. A critical assessment of the programmatic outcome is an important foundation to guide better interventions
Attribute characteristic 1.7 The plan identifies and addresses key systems issues that impact on sustainability including equity, financial and human resource and technical sustainability gaps and constraints	Interventions are described as key task under section 4 of part II of the plan	The interventions need to be clearly identified based on more in-depth (causal) analysis
	Feasibility: From a technical point of view, the current listing of interventions is not sufficient to guarantee the feasibility of the plan because concrete interventions on 'how to do' are not clearly defined	
	Appropriateness and effectiveness: Interventions presented appear to be appropriate despite the need for a greater linkage between them	
	Equity: Equity is only partially considered in the plan. In other words, it is not clear how the plan would minimise the geographical inequity in IMR and child malnutrition (Tables 1 and 2 of the plan). There is a need to refer to intersectoral action, such as education and improved female literacy rate which have a major bearing on health of children. Economic development, poverty reduction and equitable income distributions are important contribution to health equity goals	
	Sustainability: Without formal assignment of responsibility to department concerned on implementation and adequate financial commitment, it is unlikely that interventions will be sustainable	

Attribute characteristic 1.8 Plan describes short- and long-term strategies to meet technical assistance requirements for its implementation	There is no assessment on the requirement of technical assistance in the plan	Further analysis may be needed to determine which of the interventions require technical assistance
Attribute characteristic 1.9 Contingency plans for emergency health needs (natural disasters and emerging/re-emerging diseases), in line with the international health regulations, are included in national planning process at all levels	Contingent plans for emergency health needs in case of natural disaster and major disease outbreaks are still not included in the plan	Contingent plans for emerging threats, pandemics and complex emergencies need to be included or referred to if there are these plans elsewhere
Attribute 4 Both assessment of risks and proposed mitigation strategies are present and credible		
Attribute characteristic 1.10 The plan includes a risk assessment of potential barriers to successful implementation	The plan does not appear to have formal risk assessments and mitigation strategies are not well defined	Risk assessments should be addressed in draft 4 that all potential risks are well aware and plans to mitigate these risks are well thought out
	One key barrier in achieving 80 % population coverage with prepayment scheme is the contributory nature for the informal sector where enforcement and contribution collections are difficult	Risk assessment should be examined not only from health sector perspective, and risks and challenges are also examined from economical and social, natural environment perspectives
	There is a need to identify barriers and risk to achieving goals of the ten key tasks in section 4 of part II of the plan and how to mitigate these barriers	

(continued)

Dimensions and attributes	Comments on process and content	Recommendations
Dimension 2 Process soundness and inclusiveness of development and endorsement processes for the national strategy		
Attribute 5 Multi-stakeholder (including the government) involvement in development of national strategy and operational plans (led by the government, with a transparent participative process) and multi-stakeholder final endorsement of national strategy	Positive steps have been taken by MOH in adopting a new approach to planning based on openness, transparency, engaging and being more participatory	Add one section to document the process on how the plan was gradually developed to demonstrate the level of involvement and participation by stakeholders
	The application of WHO six health systems building blocks in the construct of the plan sounds reasonable and useful in strengthening health systems, the vital contribution to good health of the population	
	Genuine partnership between JAHR and planning team and efforts in involving provincial health bureaus in the plan development processes in a bottom-up manner were appreciated by key informants	
	However, only 20 % of provinces and cities submitted their provincial 5-year plan to the MOH. Influenced by the vertical nature of their programme, the level of involvement by some MOH departments is not high, with limited commitments. At times, they comment only their department's mandate without concerns over the plan as a whole. MOH officials perceive annual health plan more important than the 5-year plan	
Attribute 6 High level of political commitment (at the highest level) to national strategy	In general, key informants indicated that the plan was developed based on the direction and guideline of relevant policies, strategies and related regulations. There is verbal financial commitment by political and government agencies, but it is difficult to predict the level of annual budget and limitation of other legal frameworks	
	Integral part of the plan contributes to the development of health chapter of the national socio-economic development plan compiled and synthesised by the Ministry of Planning and Investment. This demonstrates highest-level commitments on the plan	

	The regulatory framework for developing and implementing the plan is clear. Implementation issues may arise if ownership is not present (defined as active involvement/oversight of development and adoption in day-to-day management activities) of the plan by the MOH as a whole	
Attribute 7 National strategy consistent with relevant higher- and/or lower-level strategies, financing frameworks and underlying operational plans	MOH departments, national targeted programmes and the provinces each developed their plans based on guidelines and templates provided by the DPF. These plans apply similar formats. DPF staff summarised and incorporated into the 5-year plan. However, DPF could not control the orientation and quality of these provincial plans and NTP	Full involvement by other MOH departments and NTP and reflection in the plan of subsector strategies are currently being developed. Though those strategies may not yet be completed and approved, it would be very helpful for the plan to draw on these, in order to ensure full consistency
	In a departmental plan, the national targeted programmes were developed in consistent with the national strategies and policies relevant to their areas	Further extension of consultation with ample time to allow inputs provided by a broad range of stakeholders such as professional groups, private sector and education and academic institutions
	Full involvement and contributions by provincial health bureaus are materialised when their inputs were well reflected in the plan. Bottom up ensure relevance and interrelationship between the national and subnational plans	
Dimension 2 Finance and auditing		
	Although the planning process has been robust, there is room for improvement in the linkages between the strategy, expenditure planning and resources, including with MTEF	
Attribute 8 Expenditure framework with comprehensive budget/costing of the programme areas covered by the national strategy		

(continued)

Dimensions and attributes	Comments on process and content	Recommendations
Attribute characteristic 3.1 The strategy is accompanied by a sound expenditure framework with a costed plan. It should ensure pertinent recurrent and investment financing of, e.g. human resources, access to medicines, decentralised management, infrastructures and logistics	Budget plan attached to draft 3 is not in the budget plan template that will be attached to the final version. Comments focus on the process of budget development, not on the attached budget draft	In addition to the government-defined standard format of budget plan, an additional budget table should be attached to the 5-year plan in order to clarify the JANS attributes 8 and 9
	Key informants said the budget plan was developed for all programme areas, including cost details of all systems support areas such as human resources, infrastructure, medicines and equipment and logistics. Recurrent budget is based on standard cost norm (which is always unrealistically low). But budget breakdown to each category of spending (human resources, medicines, etc.) is not clear in the budget table attached to draft 3	The 5-year budget plan should provide comprehensive coverage of central and provincial budget
	National health accounts are not widely used in development of the provincial 5-year health plan	A linkage between priority tasks and budget should be made more explicit in the budget plan
	The budget plan in draft 3 does not provide cost details of systems support areas such as human resources, infrastructure, medicines and equipment and logistics	Budget scenarios in areas of high degree of unpredictability should be provided
	There is no description of linkage between priority tasks of the plan and budget plan; therefore, there is de-linkage between priority setting and budgeting	
	Viet Nam has a very decentralised healthcare system, in which budgeting is also decentralised according to the budget law. Each province develops their own health budget proposal in line with national strategy, to be approved by the Provincial People's Council. The multiyear budget has been developed for the decentralised structures (provincial health sector). The MOH budget plan consists of budget of NTP, all its departments, health facilities and institutions under the MOH jurisdiction. The current draft budget does not show details of budgets for provincial health systems	

	As required by the Prime Minister in Directive N. 751 on the 5-year SEDP preparation, MOF sent very detailed budgeting and reporting templates and guidelines to all sectors, including health sector, for development of the plan. The 5-year health budget plan (not yet attached to draft 3) is based on the log frame sent to all provinces and all MOH departments	
	Not all provincial health departments sent back the log frame with filled-in budget information. MOH does not have adequate information regarding annual plans, budgets and resource allocation of provinces	
	MOH also used expenditure data from MOF. The provincial financial reports (standard template) are submitted to MOF by October each year	
	Key information reports that different budget scenarios for areas of high level of uncertainty were not prepared (not common in current practice) and cannot be found in the current budget plan (draft 3)	
Attribute 9 'Expenditure framework includes financial gap analysis – including a specification of known financial pledges against the budget from key domestic and international funding sources (specification of sources of domestic funds desirable)'		

(continued)

Dimensions and attributes	Comments on process and content	Recommendations
Attribute characteristic 3.2 Revenue projections are based upon explicit assumptions, include all sources of finance (local and external) and account for any foreseen uncertainties or risks	There was calculation of revenue projections, based on estimated allocation of government funding. No calculations on revenue from health insurance have been provided and discussed, neither analysis of revenue by low-, medium- and high-funding scenarios	Provide estimate of revenue from other sources especially health insurance fund and user fee collections in different scenarios of insurance coverage
	There was a process for trying to gather data on possible revenue from government funding sources and external sources, but not from health insurance funds, where by law, universal coverage should be achieved by 2014. Missing funding from VSS is a major weakness of this section	Provide calculations of potential revenue on a multiyear period by source, with beginning and periods for each source of funding
	Calculations of potential revenue for a multiyear period by source are not provided in the current budget plan	Provide analysis on bed-based government budget allocation and suggest more advanced options
	At the provincial level (Hanoi as an example), only revenue from government budget is reflected in overall revenue projections, no other sources provided	
	Government budget allocated for recurrent healthcare budget is based on capitation principle (according to the Prime Minister Decision No. 151/2006/QD- TTg and N. 219/2006/QDD-TTG)	
	Recurrent budget for each hospital is based on the number of beds given in hospitals, whilst recurrent budget for preventive care is estimated based on capitation formulae	
Attribute characteristic 3.3 Ensure health financing systems that avoid catastrophic healthcare expenditure and impoverishment from result of seeking care	Health insurance law ensured most the poor, and ethnic minorities living in disadvantaged areas (about 15 million persons in 2009) are covered by health insurance scheme through full subsidies by the government	Develop policy/strategy to ensure coverage of the near-poor and informal sector
	The near-poor households are eligible by compulsory health insurance scheme, with 50 % premium subsidised by government budget, but there is no effective mechanism to increase high level of enrolment and results in adverse selection; members have higher utilisation and are chronically ill	Develop policy and strategy to discourage the informal payment, setting the maximum of ceiling of copayment preventing catastrophic health expenditure and impoverishment. Develop policy/strategy to achieve universal coverage

	There is no suggestion on how to achieve universal coverage of health insurance by 2014, as stipulated in the health insurance law	
	High level of informal payment as well as unlimited copayment under current health insurance policy is likely to result in impoverishment from seeking care	
Attribute characteristic 3.4 Costing and budget estimates for scaling up equitable services are based on sound economic analysis	There is neither economic analysis nor costing and budgeting estimate for scaling up key programme activities	Include economic analysis and cost models for scaling up priority programmes
Attribute 10 Description of financial management system (including financial reporting against budgeted costs and accounting policies and processes) and evidence that it is adequate, accountable and transparent	The country PFM generally meets the requirements, but moderate to substantial risk exists. The 5-year plan partially meets the disclosure requirement of JANS as it does not yet have discussions regarding the finance and audit aspects. Some improvements can be introduced in the plan and the applicable FM arrangements be discussed and references made to relevant specific regulations and other existing documents	Health financing and audit section needs to be included in the document. It could discuss ways to expand the health resource base and its management in the future taking into account current and future developments in health financing. For instance, it could provide ways to guide nongovernment resources to attain national health goals. It could include alternative health financing options. The information thus generated could be used to plan the effective use of those resources
Attribute characteristic 3.5 Financial plans have transparent criteria governing allocation of funds across programmes, including subnational levels and non-state actors (where appropriate)	Financial allocation criteria across subnational levels are fairly well defined and known to all (via Prime Minister's letter). Resource allocation negotiations between sectors take place at the provincial level and transparent mechanisms are used	The government may wish to consider a contractual arrangement in order to ensure that the national strategy and priorities are consistently applied at lower levels, and the allocation of resources reflects those priorities
	Since the provinces are fully independent, their prioritisation may defer from the national priorities for the health sector	

(continued)

Dimensions and attributes	Comments on process and content	Recommendations
Attribute characteristic 3.6 Financial management system meets national and international standards as well as produces reports appropriate for decision-making, oversight and analysis	Meets substantially the national and partially international standards. The spending units produce quarterly and annual reports within reasonable time. The MOH central unit consolidates those reports annually, albeit 11 months after the end of the FY – Financial Management System – which substantially meets the national standards and is in turn partially consistent with the international standards of reporting. It does not seem to systematically produce management reports but rather ad hoc and as requested. The MOH consolidates the annual reports 11 months after the end of the FY which is slightly later than the national requirement but below international standards. There seems to be also a difference between the spending units accounting principle and the treasury (the former is modified cash/modified accrual and the latter is cash basis) that needs to be understood and resolved	As suggested above, the plan should establish clear responsibilities for financial reporting and needs in terms of frequency and content of the reports for each level and the compilation/consolidation process and responsibilities
Attribute characteristic 3.7 Sufficient staff capacity and skills to provide oversight, detect and prevent unauthorised use of funds at all levels	Meets substantially in light of the treasury staff function and capacity – the financial instructions are clear and the segregation of duties between the spending units and the treasury which handles funds is in general a robust control. On the other hand, we concluded that the 'internal audit' exists only partially	We suggest that, in consultation with the central ministries, the plan provides clear internal audit framework and procedures that deters mismanagement and ensures detection of internal control weaknesses
	The 'internal audit' can be considered as only very partially existent. It takes the form of annual verification by staff from the MOF verifying the annual reports and random checking of expenditures. There are several other controls by different organs of government, but the effectiveness is not evident	
Attribute characteristic 3.8 Sufficient staff capacity and core competencies to ensure efficient disbursement to all levels and, where appropriate, to different implementing partners	The reconciliation between the spending units and the payments by the national treasury has been reported to be problematic across the sectors and provinces. However, we were informed that this is done correctly and monthly by MOH and DOHs in provinces	This issue deserves further review at the spending units at the provincial level as the health sector would be a good model for other sectors and the use of the national system would become a real possibility for the health sector, should the reconciliation be practised on a monthly basis

Attribute characteristic 3.9 There are formal and systematic mechanisms to ensure timely disbursements and identify fund flow bottlenecks and resolve them	It is not clear how the treasury staff prioritise payments in periods of cash shortfalls and competing demands for payment (e.g. between paying salaries or the suppliers)	This is also an area for further review at the provincial and district level at the treasury units. No systematic mechanism to identify bottlenecks and their resolution were reported
Attribute 11 Description of audit procedures and evidence of appropriate scope of audit work, as well as independence and capacity of auditors	Country situation partially meets the requirements; the plan is silent on the subject	
Attribute characteristic 3.10 There are effective fiduciary processes, as evidenced by routine internal and external audits of financing, procurement and resource management at all administrative levels	Meeting partially, the external audit is performed by the SAV every other year providing partial audit; the internal audit is done once a year before the consolidated financial reports are issued. This is also considered as very partial internal audit. The procurement risk has been assessed by the World Bank and by other DPs [progress towards the use of country system seems to have stalled – to be completed]	The external financial audit would need to become annual without any audit gap and be complemented with 'value for money' and procurement audits; the role and attributes of the inspectorates and verification bodies need to be better clarified in the laws. We recommend that the use of carefully selected qualified private sector auditors be considered as complement to the SAV audits
Attribute characteristic 3.11 Independence, authority, skills and competencies of auditors meet national and international standards	Partially adequate, the capacity and competency of SAV auditors have been improving but still partial	The external financial audit would need to become annual without any audit gap and be complemented with 'value for money' and procurement audits; the role and attributes of the inspectorates and verification bodies need to be better clarified in the laws. We recommend that the use of carefully selected qualified private sector auditors be considered as complement to he SAV audits
Attribute characteristic 3.12 Audit system which assures performance is routinely assessed against 'value for money'	Partially adequate, the capacity and competency of SAV auditors have been improving but still partial	Many private sector audit firms have good capacity and comply with the international standards. As an interim measure, they can be used to complement the SAVs' capacity

(continued)

Dimensions and attributes	Comments on process and content	Recommendations
Attribute characteristic 3.13 A parliamentary or other public account auditing committee credibly investigate alleged irregularities. Appropriate sanctions are applied	Meeting very partially, the SAV does from time to time include in its work the performance angle, whilst its audits are mainly planned as performance and financial	Given the workload of SAV and level of staffing, the SAV could subcontract the audit work to private auditors, under its responsibility. Moving forwards, and as an interim measure, we recommend that this type of audit for DPs be contracted out to private auditors
Attribute 12 In the context of national development policies (where applicable) – explanation of how external resources will be channelled, managed and reported on – description of relevant domestic financing policies (in relation to different approaches to resource pooling), if relevant, and description of how fiscal space constraints to scaling up spending will be managed	The plan partially meets the JANS criteria both in terms of describing the internal financial arrangements and flows and the fiscal space constraints	
Attribute characteristic 3.14 Plan clearly describes all internal financial arrangements and funding modalities and how internal and external funds will be channelled, managed and reported on	The plan does not describe	The finance and auditing section would need to be added as per JANS guidelines
	Whilst on-budget resources are discussed, planned and monitored, there are external resources that flow directly to some provinces. Allocation of these resources is not transparent. As a result, there could be duplication of efforts. Similarly, fund flows from households are not well known. Whether or not such resources contribute towards attaining national health goals is not clear	The DPs who directly provide funding are advised to disclose fully their contributions and the priorities they are aiming. The plan should attempt to include 'all resources' on or off budget and try to map resources to priorities and expenditures and develop scenarios showing how/where would potential additional funding be directed for scaling up
Attribute characteristic 3.15 The plan has explicit guidance on how programmes will manage fiscal space constraints to scaling up	Meets very partially. Plans to overcome fiscal space constraints are not in place	The document would need to discuss beyond budgetary resources

Dimension 3 Financing and auditing: cross-cutting		
Dimension 3 Strengths	The 5-year plan highlights resource inadequacy and revenue shortfall for which funding source is not known	
	There is increasingly a transparent process and criteria for allocation of resources. Workshops and consultations have been organised to reach consensus for allocation of resources in 4 categories of provinces (namely, in urban area, plain area, mountainous-minority ethnic residential area, highland and island area)	
	The costing of all activities is presented in a useful and easy-to-understand manner	
	The PFM system has a strong separation between the budget holder and payment system in the treasury system which controls and if legitimate makes payments. The budget holders do not receive funds or make payments directly (except for the DP projects with PMUs and designated accounts exist)	
	Many years of detail planning and several years of MTEF piloting and other public financial management reforms under implementation by the GOV have already benefited the sector (e.g. TABMIS deployed in about 35 provinces and the central MOH with plans going forwards to complete full deployment by the end of 2011)	
	Despite the fact that the plan document doesn't include much on financial management and audit, as expected by JANS guidelines, the planning process has been very robust	
	With the results from many studies and workshops/exercises, weaknesses and issues related to financial planning are known to the management which would help their resolution	

(continued)

Dimensions and attributes	Comments on process and content	Recommendations
Dimension 3 Weaknesses	Although the planning process has been robust, there is room for improvement in the linkages between the strategy, expenditure planning and resources, including with MTEF	Health financing and audit section needs to be included in the document in a succinct manner with reference to other documents which have more specific details. It could discuss ways to expand the health resource base and its management in the future taking into account current and future developments in health financing. For instance, it could provide ways to guide nongovernment resources to attain national health goals. It could include alternative health financing options. The information thus generated could be used to plan the effective use of those resources
	The plan document does not have enough description or cross reference to other documents regarding financial management and audit. The health financing and audit section needs to be expanded and adequate reference be made to other existing documents	A discussion on the interlinkages between HSDP, health financing strategy and the health insurance expansion and how they interact would be useful
	Alternative government and nongovernment financing options are not adequately discussed. The plan should have adequate analysis and discussion of such options	There is a need to provide a road map for resource generation and allocation based on clear and realistic assumptions. Alternatively, if optimistic assumptions are made, the document could list the ways to get there
	MOH does not have adequate information regarding annual plans, budgets and resource allocation of provinces. This is a weakness for management decision-making that would be resolved once the MOH is given access in TABMIS. The same comment applies to the reporting on the budget execution, due to delayed reporting and consolidation of information	Various future health financing scenarios need to be considered in the light of certain new developments including the growth of the GDP, population, aging and nongovernment funding mechanisms

	Analysis concerning health financing is not effectively linked with priorities and targets. The section on health financing describes shortcomings, but no suggestion and alternative options to overcome has been given; the linkages and solutions to overcome the shortcomings are critical. We haven't been given any material on this issue other than the 3rd draft of the 5-year HSDP	Scalable health financing experiments and other health financing means such as domestic philanthropic resources could be attracted and tracked so as to streamline them or scale them up for their wider and targeted use
	Resource prioritisation is unclear whether it will be based on the resource envelope or what is achievable within a time span of 5 years. The HSDP seems to have followed an 'arithmetic approach' compiling all the resource needs rather than a consolidation or 'chemical approach' wherein different resource options and needs are well synthesised into a single plan for the sector. More analysis and clarifications are advisable	Household out-of-pocket spending is mentioned as a health financing challenge. But the document does not provide any strategy to overcome the challenge. It will be useful if the document provides an action plan to minimise the household reliance on the out-of-pocket spending to finance healthcare. It could spell out how these resources could be channelled using the existing or to-be-developed prepayment mechanisms
	Internal and external audits do not provide a full scope reasonable assurance on a timely manner, nor do they look at 'value for money' aspect. The systematic skipping of audit of every other financial year by SAV increases the fiduciary risk. The MOH, in consultation with others (SAV, MOF, DPs), should establish a workable audit framework which satisfies the need for reasonable assurance to all financiers. The document should elaborate on the audit framework	
Dimension 4 Implementation and management		
Attribute 13 'Operational plans are regularly developed through a participatory process, and detail strategic plan objectives will be achieved'		

(continued)

Dimensions and attributes	Comments on process and content	Recommendations
Attributable characteristic		
4.1 Roles and responsibilities of implementing partners are described for each strategy and intervention	Roles and responsibilities of implementation partners are not clearly proposed in the plan, and it is hard to assess how ten key tasks would be successfully implemented	
4.2 Each strategic objective has measurable annual milestones to assess progress towards implementation	There are no clear milestones for each strategy/intervention presented	
Attribute 14 'Description of how resources will be deployed to achieve clearly defined outcomes'		
Attributable characteristic		
4.3 The organisation of service delivery is defined and identifies equitable allocation of resources (recurrent investments) by the level of care and roles and responsibilities of service providers, including plans for referrals and supervision	In the implementation section of the draft 3, it is not clear how financial/human resources will be deployed to achieve clearly defined outcomes. It is assumed from the experience in implementing the previous plan 2006–2010 that the resource gap is not significant	Should have a section to describe and discuss on resource deployment from national and international sources
4.4 Human resource (management and capacity) needs are identified, including staffing levels, skill mix, training, supervision and incentives. Gaps needed to implement the national strategy are identified and a plan provided to solve identified gaps		
4.5 Current logistics, information and management system constraints are described, and credible actions are put in place to resolve constraints		

Attribute 15 Procurement policy that complies with international guidelines and evidence of adequate, accountable, and transparent procurement and supply management systems with capacity to reach target populations		
Attribute 16 'Specification of governance, management and co-ordination mechanisms for implementation'	Governance management and co-ordination are not clearly defined in the plan; there is no specific reference to who are held responsible for each of the specific objectives, central versus the provincial, district and commune levels. In other words, the accountability arrangement is non-existent	
Dimension 5 Results, monitoring and review		
Attribute 17 Plan for M&E that includes clearly described output and outcome/impact indicators, with related multiyear targets that can be used to measure progress and make performance-based decision	The M&E section of the plan is very modest compared to other sections. Totally, there are 19 basic indicators which are categorised into input, process and outcome. Selected indicators are presented as follows:	The current set of indicators and targets should be expanded to capture the whole process (from input to impact) as much as possible and incorporate the left-out areas. More specifically, as suggested by the HPG, 'the set of indicators could be strengthened by being made more specific and tailored to national needs and stratified (e.g. geographically) to incorporate inequity'. HPG also suggested the following areas be better covered: equity, efficiency, safety, effectiveness, quality, compliance with diagnostic/service protocol indicators, pharmaceuticals, NCD, communicable diseases, injuries, newborn health, maternal and child nutrition, TB (see more specific information in comments from HPG)

(continued)

Dimensions and attributes	Comments on process and content	Recommendations
	Input indicators: proportion of bed/10,000 people; proportion of physician/pharmacist/10,000 people; proportion of CHC having a physician/nurse.	In order to develop a good set of indicators that can summarise the M&E plan, it is important to develop a logical frame that describes clearly objectives and interventions selected and then input, process, output, outcome and impact indicators
	Process indicators: proportion of CHS meeting national benchmark standards, coverage of health insurance, etc.	The following include some of the indicators we suggest to be classified into the set of indicators:
	Outcome/impact indicators: infant mortality rate; population growth rate; maternal mortality rate; prevalence of HIV; life expectancy at birth	Health status: under-five malnutrition rate (height for age – stunning)
	All indicators are divided into multiyear targets for the whole period to measure progress and performance	Effectiveness of curative and preventive measures: AIDS mortality rate per 100 000 population; TB incidence rate (AFB+) per 100,000 population; Dengue fever incidence; average length of stay; proportion of detected hypertensive peopled get treated
	The indicators were developed based on (i) the party's documents and government's strategies or national plans; (ii) annually targeting indicators designated by the national assembly; (iii) the MDG indicators; (iv) achievements of the 2006–2010 period; (v) orientations for the development of socio-economics for the 2010–2020 period proposed in the draft document of the National Party Congress XI (Official of DPF); and (vi) references from other developing countries with similar socio-economic conditions	Quality of human resources: proportion of health workers with university and higher education; proportion of doctors licenced (required by the law of examination and treatment)

	In order to develop health indicators, the DPF carried out several steps as follows: (i) conducted an assessment of the achievement of health indicators in the previous plan (2006–2010); (ii) sent proposed indicators and multiyear targets measuring progress to all related departments and asked for comments; (iii) consolidated all comments and feedback and sent the proposed indicators back to the related departments for second comment if they have; and (iv) organised a meeting with MPI (Department of Labour and Social Affair and Department of Synthesising) and the National Assembly (the Committee for Social Affair) and then finalised a set of health indicators (the document No. 5597/BYT-KHTC, dated August 20, 2010)	Pharmaceutical industry: proportion of pharmaceutical manufacturers given GMP/GLP/GSP-WHO certificate; proportion of pharmacies given GPP certificate
	The proposed indicators are related to the following aspects: population; human resources; primary healthcare; health financing; preventive medicine; and maternal and child health. However, it is important to note that the proportion of indicators falling into population and human resources aspects account for more than 50 % of total indicators	Health spending: proportion of state health expenditures spent on preventive medicine and out-of-pocket payment
	There were no indicators related to food safety, infectious and non-communicable diseases, quality of care; health information system; pharmaceutical industry; large investment programmes (i.e. Decision No. 930), although they are considered key focuses. As a result, it is difficult, if not impossible, to measure progress and performance of prioritised actions listed in the plan using the proposed set of indicators	More indicators could be found in NTP and other national strategies

(continued)

Dimensions and attributes	Comments on process and content	Recommendations
	In-depth interview with an official at DPF revealed a couple of reasons for selecting 19 indicators: 'These indicators are most common and representative the potential impact. If we selected the indicators that are too specific, we may not able to collect them from all provinces. More importantly, these indicators can be monitored and evaluated easily. It is impossible for indicators to be selected if they are not evaluated or we do not have baseline information, i.e. qualitative indicators. To some extent, these indicators could be considered targets from which specific programs and its performance indicators such as proportion of people at risk using bed- net… would be developed and implemented'. Other justifications supporting for not detailing the M&E is that 'this 5 year plan should be seen as a guiding document from which specific programs will be developed with detailed indictors by in-charge Department or Institutions. Moreover, many indicators such as quality of care, financial management are not measurable'	A regular performance analysis should be officially in place
	A JAHR team member thought that 'it is important to emphasize that the 19 selected indicators serve the national 5-year plan. They could not adequately reflect performance of the health sector. A full list of indicators for the 5-year plan would be as large as ten folds'	The JAHR process could be further developed, in order to serve the purpose of joint annual monitoring process (which would also have to draw from an internal monitoring process set-up)
	A regular performance analysis was not found in the plan, but it's mentioned when interviewing health officials	
	The JAHR indicator recommendations, which were developed in a consultative process, do not appear to have been included in the plan. Currently, JAHR is not an M&E of the Plan. 'If JAHR was a tool for M&E of the Plan, it would have been done differently. Now, the two are different. Therefore, the plan should have a separate M&E section and indicators representing each activity, while JAHR still focuses on crucial issues of the health sector' (IDI with JAHR team member)	

	Health officials understand very well about the M&E and its indicators. They acknowledged that these selected indicators are not adequate and more should be added. However, they gave several reasons for not selecting all related indicators, for example, 'it could create a huge workload while we do not have time, human resource and finance'	
Attribute 18 Plan for M&E that includes sources of information for indicators and description of information flows	The M&E section includes sources of information for each indicator and ranges from epidemiological data, routine HIS, census and Viet Nam living standard survey	For some indicator such as infant mortality rate and under-5 mortality rate, there are two sources of information including census and routine health information system. It is important to keep an eye on the results reported by these sources in case there is discrepancy between two sources
	With respect to indicators collected by the MOH through the routine HIS, in 2009, the MOH issued a Decision No. 3440/ QD- BYT promulgating a standardised health statistics reporting formats. These standardised data collection tools ensure that data collected is logically linked to one-third of the selected M&E indicators at all levels and on a routine basis (3, 6 and 9 months), although quality of this data is still debatable	To serve as a good reference document for the M&E section, it would be very important to reconsider the role of JAHR. It would also be crucial to review the set of indicators developed for the JAHR to make sure that the adaptation into the 5-year plan is legitimate. This is also a comment from HPG: 'Though it is mentioned that the JAHR are used as a reference source to assess annual health sector performance, it is not stated that the JAHR will be used as a basis for jointly monitoring the implementation of the plan. It is essential, therefore, that the role of the JAHR be further clarified and redefined in the context of M&E of the Plan'
	For M&E plan indicators that cannot be monitored from a routine basis such as infant mortality rate, life expectancy and maternal mortality rate, information from census will be applied	
	The M&E plan specified the role of related organisations in collecting and reporting the selected indicators following the regulations on the national set of indicators. It also stated that the M&E framework proposed in the JAHR conducted by the MOH under support from the Health Partnership Group will be used complimentarily for the M&E plan	
	There was no information gap reported, and we found it adequate. However, this might be an issue if more indicators are added	

(continued)

Dimensions and attributes	Comments on process and content	Recommendations
Attribute 19 Plan for M&E that includes descriptions of data collection/data management methods, tools and analytical processes (including quality assurance)	The M&E describes information source but not methods of data collection for each indicator. In fact, it assigned responsibilities to related organisations to collect data and reporting. It is assumed that these in-charge organisations will be responsible for managing and conducting data analysis. As there are several data sets such as routine HIS and census, data collection, management and analysis would vary and be out of reach of the MOH	Given that more indicators will be selected, details of roles and responsibilities of related stakeholders should be specified and stated in the 5-year plan
	The JANS team felt that data from national survey or census would be in good quality and that quality control is well in place, whilst information from the routine HIS collected from public facilities only would be inadequate as private sectors play an increasing role in service provisions	
	Comments from HPG revealed that: 'Information currently reported can be unreliable and internally inconsistent. Denominators are inappropriate (e.g. coverage based on attendances not population'; numerators are incorrect (e.g. not all infant deaths are fully counted); sources are inappropriate (e.g. hospital source for incidence/prevalence data) and there are perverse incentives for over-reporting. There is no systematic data definition, collection, data processing, independent validation, reporting and use. The issue of independent validation is particularly important)'. Even an official at the MOH admitted that 'number of maternal deaths reported from public hospitals is not correct because a lot of patients were discharged before death, and died at home'	
	Information from the routine HIS is collected quarterly from commune to district, from district to province and from provincial to central level – the MOH. As mentioned above about the Decision No. 3440/QD-BYT, there was a very detailed guideline on how health information is collected and reported from the commune level to central level	

	It should be noted that, 'Quality of information collected from the routine HIS is not very good. However, it varies from one to another indicator'	
Attribute 20 There is a plan for join periodic performance review (reporting of results against specific objectives and respective targets explaining any deviations) and processes for the development of related corrective measures	The M&E section described how performance will be monitored over time. Specifically, the National Assembly will carry out an M&E annually over the indicators designated to the health sector; the MOH will be responsible for M&E the overall performance of the health sector under support of the Health Partnership Group through the Joint Assessment of Health Report. Finally, provincial departments of health will be responsible for M&E the performance of the health sector within their province	It is suggested that not all indictors are evaluated at the same time, for example, input and process indicators should be evaluated or monitored annually, whilst output indicators should be evaluated at least after 2 years of the implementation of the plan
	Outputs of these activities are comprised of JAHR, M&E report of the National Assembly and annual performance report of the Provincial Department of Health	
	Although the M&E did not mention about using of feedback on performance, we did find a two-way feedback mechanism in which information flows to central level and back to those providing them. For example, the National Assembly will keep the MOH informed about their M&E activities on the indicators they assigned to the health sector. At provincial level, the M&E is implemented quarterly. 'Currently (October) we are asking the organizations to report their performance within the first 9 months and submit the following year plan. All organizations have to provide justifications for changes in the plan in the following year' (IDI with an official of Hanoi DOH)	
	An annual report is submitted by the Provincial Department of Health to the Provincial People's Committee and sent a copy the MOH	

(continued)

Dimensions and attributes	Comments on process and content	Recommendations
Attribute 21 M&E plan describes processes by which monitoring results can influence decision-making (including financial disbursement)	The M&E section did not describe how the outcome is formally incorporated into future reorientation of policy decisions. But officials at MOH and Provincial Department of Health emphasised the importance of the annual performance assessment reports. 'The budget and plan targets can be adjusted after 9 months implementation. If responsible agencies found that they could not meet the designated targets, they would propose for adjustments' (IDI with an official at provincial DOH)	
	Usually, an annual performance assessment is conducted in September to report how the plan was carried, what indicators are achieved and which activity and budget would be added in the following year	

Index

A.G. Shillabeer, *The Health of Vietnam*, DOI 10.1007/978-981-287-709-3

The manufacturer's authorised representative in the EU is Springer Nature Customer Service Centre GmbH, Europaplatz 3, 69115 Heidelberg, Germany. If you have any concerns regarding our products, please contact ProductSafety@springernature.com

Printed and bound by CPI Group (UK) Ltd, Croydon, CR0 4YY
30/09/2026
02225436-0018